TAKE 10

You Are Only
Ten Seconds Away
From A
Human Connection

Kevin L. Barclay

Taking Ten to
Talk About Take 10

"Kevin's work and words shine through with the simple message that we all should practice, be kind to one another. His passion for life jumps off the pages."

Jamie Hamilton, AAI ARM CPCU
Home Loan
Chairman and CEO

"I enjoyed the relaxed writing style. I see value for those who may have a general sense of wanting to make changes in their personal or professional lives to help them communicate more effectively, improve relationships, and experience more peace. Thank you for sharing this book with me. It raised my personal mindfulness and gave me some things to think about."

Amy Kulp, M.S.
Washington, DC

"Kevin has developed a simple and effective method to improve the quality of your life through the *Take 10* method."

Anna D.
Graduating class 2018
Grand Junction High School

Between stimulus and response there is a space.
In that space is our power to choose our response.
In our response lies our growth and our freedom.

—Victor E. Frankl

Dedication

This book is dedicated to my loving wife, April, and to my children: Kevin, Chris, Adam, and RubyJean. You are my heart!

To my extended family, Kathryn, my mother-in-law; Rachel and Crystal and their families.

To Terry, my father-in-law, and his inspiration to be a better man. I miss you!

To my siblings Sean, Erin and Colleen may this book help create more closure for us.

———

And to my **MusE** (Marty Ealey). Without you, this book would not exist. No words can express my gratitude and appreciation. You are the angel on my shoulder.

———

My Support Team	**Mentors**
Eugene Slocum	Mike Ferris
Danelle Ridenour	Berry Fowler
Rocky, Lewis, Paul	

———

Bill and Steve Harrison
QuantumLeap Publicity and
Marketing Program Team

For information about this title or to order other books and/or electronic media, contact the publisher:

Begreat44Publishing
2139 North 12th Street #7
Grand Junction, CO 81506
taking10.org
Begreat44@yahoo.com

Library of Congress Control Number: pending

ISBN: 978-1-7323771-2-7 (Print)
        978-1-7323771-3-4 (E-book)

Printed in the United States of America
Cover and Interior design: 1106 Design

Meet the Author

Kevin's rich blend of experiences and talent allows him a unique approach to life and its many mysteries, allowing him to connect through his words and thoughts. As a prison guard, a stand-up comedian, and with three decades of sales, sales managing, sales training, marketing, and more, he has a different perspective and the ability to reach through the pages and touch your heart. As a life coach, author, and motivational speaker, his passion is to encourage, uplift, and inspire.

"Kevin has a unique approach in discussing issues that make it seem like he is talking to each individual person. We laughed… we cried."

Kathryn Thomas, RN
Staff Development Coordinator
Larchwood Inns
Grand Junction, CO

"Kevin was able to make my staff laugh and cheer in a way that was very motivating."

Cole Christianson
General Manager
Gold's Gym
Grand Junction, CO

"Kevin's BE GREAT presentation to our staff was very helpful. One staff member with more than 15 years' tenure said, 'It changed how I think about my job.'"

Wade McDowell
Assistant Administrator
Family Health West
Fruita, CO

Contact him at
Healing Horizons, 2139 N. 12th Street
Grand Junction, CO
970-985-8591
begreat44@yahoo.com

Table of Contents

Introduction

As I sit in my office and look at the books up on the shelf and think of all the motivational speakers whom I have either heard or read, I realize these authors all have communicated wonderful information. The speakers are amazing and highly motivated and have great messages. I think about which one I would grab if I needed encouragement or uplifting. All these books require a fair amount of time to study and practice techniques, etc. I am writing this book because I believe the answer is so simple it seems hard. I want to make it less complicated.

The overall significance of this book and what I am looking to accomplish is to point out that maybe it *is* that simple. Maybe all we have to do is *hit the pause button*. Maybe all we have to do is "just relax, slow down, and enjoy our shoes" a quote from *Hitchhiker's Guide to the Galaxy*, an interesting cult film whose main premise is

1

"Don't panic." We all need to just relax, not take ourselves so seriously, and *Take 10.* Remember when you were perhaps just a little overheated, your mom used to say, "Count to 10"?

Well, that's what we might all need, with the world seeming to spin as fast as it is now and with all the different things going on. Maybe we just need to *Take 10*—maybe take *10 breaths, 10 steps.* We **are** *10 seconds* away from making a better decision! Many people have said that a situation could have turned out differently had they paused and given it more thought.

This book will help you continue on the interesting journey you have already begun. This is a guide to help you understand that you already have the tools inside you to do what you need to take care of yourself. You already have the basis of understanding. You already have everything you need at your fingertips. You don't have to recite any mantras or anything; you just have to remember to *take it easier.*

The chapters in this book are unique, and each represents a thought I have been mulling over for years. You've all heard the expression, "Those who cannot do, teach." This is an interesting concept. If you take it literally, it means that even if you can't do something, you can teach it. As the teachers instruct repeatedly, they will become masters of the technique. Therefore, I'm hoping to become a true master of the techniques mentioned in this book.

I hope this book will give you a fresh and insightful look at ways you can deal with people in stressful situations. The chapters "Benefit of the Doubt" and "Self-Talk" deal with your response to other people—things that you say to yourself or things you can give yourself as little reminders not to respond in the wrong way. Listening is another tool that provides you a way to respond. If you apply the three little tips on how easy it is to be a better active listener you will see how it works for you.

The "Genius Gift" chapter is one of my favorites. All of us have this special *genius gift* inside. The "Snap-Back Effect" chapter addresses a simple, common phenomenon: fad diets work for a while, but then most people regain the weight they lost—plus 15 or 20 pounds more. I'm that guy. You know how frustrating that is! You remember the days of weight-loss success, but the reality is that it was too much, too fast. This happens with other habits we try to overcome all at once—goals we think can be accomplished in one fell swoop. In each instance we are at risk for the snap-back effect. Slow and steady is a better way to achieve any goal.

The movie *What About Bob?* is a story about a guy who has obsessive-compulsive disorder. The solution for him was all about taking baby steps. Like Bill Murray did in the movie, we can actually learn as we go—just to take little steps, not big strides. If you take a big, long step, you might find yourself seriously off balance.

The second half of the book includes something I have worked on for years—how to BE GREAT. This is an acronym for **bravery in leadership, encouragement,** and **gratitude** for what you have and not longing for what you don't; having **respect** for your next-door neighbor and **empathy** for the situation he is facing. Being **adaptable** when faced with **adversity**—whatever happened to being flexible and adapting to our surroundings? We seem to force everything to fit us the way *we* want it! Rounding out the acronym are most importantly **time** and **trust**: Taking time to be with one another, putting the phones down, looking into someone's eyes, and hearing what they have to say. *Take 10!* Choose yourself, and *take it easy.*

My reasons for writing a book like this go back a long way. When I was around seven years old, in the morning my brother and sisters and I would pretend that we were asleep when my dad left for work. Then we would all hide when my father came home. I would hear him mixing his cocktail and could tell by the sound how the evening would go. I was probably more aware when I was older than seven, but that is when the beatings began. My father would regularly come after us—maybe because of a shoe left in the middle of the room or something left on the couch at night. The reason didn't seem to matter. In his mind, we had always done something punishable.

The spanking and hitting and choking and slapping and pushing—they all grew tiresome. I recall watching my brother get hurt—one time he was hit so hard that he slid down the hallway and was covered with feces; it was a horrible night! I was naïve as I was growing up. I had no idea about the things happening with my two sisters behind closed doors. I did not know then, but unfortunately I know now. As a teen, I worked out really hard so I could get strong enough to be able to beat my father up. He passed away when I was 18 years old, and I have to say that, more than anything, I was relieved.

While all this was happening, my mother just stood by. Two years after my father's death, she entered a mental-health facility; 28 years later she died, after having been in either a mental-health facility or a full-care facility the whole time. She never drove a car, loved another man, or cooked a meal again. For 28 years, she stayed hidden away after my father died; then she passed away—never apologizing, never answering questions that were asked, never really giving us any idea of how she felt, never giving us any closure.

I'm not going to sit here and complain about the life I've had. I have a beautiful wife, four beautiful children, and, at my age of 61, my 7-year-old twins are just amazing. The idea of *Taking 10* is something that is contagious. Just ask my daughter, who tells me, whenever she sees me getting upset, "*Take 10*, Daddy. *Take 10!*"

I'm really just like you. When you picked up this book, you were looking for an answer. Socrates said, "It is not really knowing the answers but knowing the right questions." He also said, "Wisdom begins in wonder."

I have learned to ask the right questions. Why do kids get abused? Why is the entire world having all these problems? Why are these things happening in the world? Why is it that neighbors don't talk to each other or sit on the porch anymore? Why are our suicide rates increasing among the young? Why is it that marriages fall apart? Why do relationships die? Why do we spend so much time on the computer, on the Internet, or on our iPhones or other portable devices?

The answers to these questions may be so simple that it is hard to believe. Maybe we have become too preoccupied to accept it or believe it. Maybe we lose that ability. Maybe *taking 10* is the answer to all of those questions—when we *take 10 seconds* to make a better decision, we *take 10 deep breaths* when we have a problem, and we *take 10 steps* away from a confrontation we do not need to have with someone.

In the first five chapters, we are going to examine how we deal with ourselves on the inside, and the next seven chapters will discuss how we interact with one another, including "BE GREAT" (bravery in leadership/ encouragement, having gratitude, respect, empathy, being adaptable in adversity, taking time, and learning to trust). We *take time* to appreciate people. We *take time* to love one another. We *Take 10* to make sure we have the patience to do it.

What you will find in here are tips that are just to remind you what you already know! You already know the answers to your questions. You know how to take care of all these things. It is all inside of you. You just have to reach in and touch it, but you cannot do that if you are in a hurry all the time! You're driving fast. At the same time, you're eating and putting on makeup and trying to discipline your child in the backseat for using crayons and writing on the seats. You don't have time for all that, so you have to *Take 10—before* you discipline your child, *before* you yell at your spouse, *before* you storm out of your office, and *before* you make those good, bad, ugly, or indifferent remarks to a coworker. The benefits for you of *Taking 10* are real.

Top-of-mind awareness—constant recognition of what your goals are—is one of the most important skills you can ever develop. *Take the time* to do the things that are really important to you. Will reading this book change your life? I don't know, but it could affect your life. It could make your life just a little bit easier, and it could encourage you.

I asked people to sum up in two words a message they would share with the whole world if they could. Their responses included, "Love God," "Love yourself," "Be fun, have fun," and "Be kind." The predominant messages were, "Slow down," "Loosen up," "Be mindful."

This book will make it easier for you to remind yourself to *Take 10*. The benefits are clear and easy to understand. The chapters may be shorter than in many other books, but they will also be very poignant. You don't need to spend your life reading a book, but you should learn to *Take 10* whenever you need to for the rest of your life. You should be able to "relax and enjoy your shoes," to enjoy your life and your family. You can *slow down* just a little bit, stop watching news nonstop all day long—the stock market's ups and downs, potholes, epidemics, and everything else.

You may find many benefits from embracing this book! What a wonderful gift we could give each other if we could do this! So as we go on this journey together— and I really appreciate you joining me—we will encourage each other and will learn to *Take 10*. You will look somebody in the eye rather than just glancing up as you are racing past them.

Thank you so much for picking this book. I hope you enjoy it. I know it will make a difference for you if you can just *slow down* a little and *Take 10!*

CHAPTER 1

Wise men, when in doubt whether to speak or be quiet, give themselves the benefit of the doubt and remain silent.
—NAPOLEON HILL

Benefit of the Doubt

I remember *going out* to breakfast with the whole family, and as we were walking through the front door of the restaurant, there was a lot going on. Off to the side, there was a homeless man (or I assumed he was because he was somewhat disheveled) digging through the trash. He would reach in and pull out plastic and put it in one bag, paper in another bag, and aluminum cans in another bag. He was basically separating all the trash; I assumed he could earn money by recycling the items.

We walked inside, and I was still thinking about him. He preoccupied my mind, so I had to go back out and talk to him, see him, give him something. Often we will see people standing on corners with signs asking for money, even veterans needing help. I went back to see him while the family was inside. I reached into my pocket to give him some money even though he was not asking for it. As I handed him the money, he looked at me and smiled. He had the look of an angel—he seemed touched that I gave him money. I don't think I said anything. He said, "Thank you."

I went back in and ate breakfast with my family. I thought about my interaction with this man for a long time. Even though he might have been homeless (judging by the way he looked), there was an order about him. He had all the stuff to recycle, had it separated, had a system.

So often when we look at people, we make an assessment based on their outward appearance. We look at a person and say, "He's a homeless man." We see somebody in a suit, and we assume that he is a businessman because he is dressed so well. We make assumptions from the outside without really knowing who the person is or how he might handle himself in any given situation.

In managing salespeople for nearly three decades and watching how they responded to other people, I came up with something I called the "90/10 rule." A salesperson would come to me complaining how difficult a customer was—he was angry; he was distant. As he worked with the customer, the salesperson recognized that he was just not going to get along with this particular customer and that maybe somebody else should go talk to him. It was a difficult customer, and the salesperson wanted out! I had seen that same attitude in some of the assisted-care and full-care facilities where I volunteered, giving talks to the staff and learning about how they felt disconnected from their family members.

The "90/10 rule" works like this: if you are dealing with a person in front of you and making an assessment (and we all do it because it is human nature), consider that how the person communicates with you is a result of everything that happened to this individual from the moment he or she woke up this morning, and not just you. If the individual has been having a great day, the person will be pleasant. This is not 100% accurate; there are some people who are able to transcend a difficult day and respond to others pleasantly. I applaud those people! If that's you, fantastic! The rest of us will have a response based on everything that has built up.

So, the salesman came to me and said he just could not connect with the customer—that he was really angry and upset. Often I would suggest that the salesman just imagine how the customer's day has gone. Let's assume, for instance, that maybe he has had a horrible morning. He fought with his wife, couldn't get his kids to school on time, and forgot to give them lunch money. Maybe he got pulled over and received a ticket. All of that may be reflected in the way that person responds to you when you talk to him—whether you are a salesman talking to a customer, a barista at Starbucks, a person selling mattresses, or maybe just having a chance encounter on the street—it doesn't make much difference. A person who comes to you and is really antagonistic is the total of all the things that have happened to him up to that point. The 10% you own is that you are there. How does that help us? If we give him the benefit of the doubt, we realize that, on the inside, *maybe* there is a lot of stuff that is boiling beneath the surface. We can't tell by looking at him. We see a homeless man sleeping out in a park; we see how he is dressed and make assumptions that he has had a tough time, and we hand him money. We see somebody dressed smartly, and he is angry, yelling and screaming, and we just assume he is a jerk.

What if we were to assume the best instead? What if we gave each person the benefit of the doubt? What if we could just *Take 10, hit the pause button*, and—before we actually make an assessment of who he is—we just gave *him the benefit of the doubt?* How would that help us? Often when I tell people about this way to handle a situation, they say, "Why would I want to give that person the benefit of the doubt? I don't want to let him off the hook. The guy's a jerk!" This is not about them—this is about *you*. This is about how you can respond to people. This is how you can *hit the pause button*, think about the interaction for a moment, and realize he is coming from a different place. A lot of what he is giving you—his attitude, the way he is barking at you, his inability to connect, or maybe just his distant, docile look—is based on everything that has happened to him so far today. The question of letting him off the hook is not the goal here. The goal is how we respond to him.

You may have seen someone who handles customer service perform so well that you want to stand there and applaud them. I have to admit there can be challenging customers sometimes. I've worked with people who handled things well, and I've worked with people who have handled things badly. If we can *give people the benefit of the doubt*, it does something to us inside. We remain calm and relaxed. We know he is having a difficult time. We do not reach into our pocket and give people money all the time, but we certainly can be a little more patient and understanding with them.

What really happens during that whole transaction? This person comes at you, and you know that he has to be aware of how he is acting at some point—maybe not right away but eventually. Maybe he even felt righteous indignation: "I deserve to be acting this way because I deserve the best service." He doesn't realize he is making it difficult to give him that kind of service. Again, back to you. You are *hitting the pause button* and realizing that this person has issues.

The other day I spoke at an assisted-living residence. I asked, "If there is anybody in this room who does not have a worry or concern or some burden that you carry on a day-to-day basis—whether it's family, health, income or anything else—raise your hand." When you think about it, you realize that is kind of a silly question because who would want to raise their hand and say that? At any rate, I had no takers. As I looked around the room, I realized that all of the 150 to 200 people sitting there had something on their minds. If we *allow people the benefit of the doubt* and we let them off the hook, so to speak, and we comfort and encourage them, then that could not only change that transaction (and it will keep us cool, calm, and confident during the confrontation), but it might also make a difference in their lives. They might walk away thinking, *What an incredible person that is! He or she was able to handle me in this situation and have it come out like that.* I have said that to myself sometimes when I have been a little excited, maybe a little bit put off by the way the service was, and how cool, calm, and relaxed people were when they were dealing with me. I walked away shaking my head saying to myself that I could have been a better person.

What does this phenomenon result in, and how does it benefit all of us? If you give *others the benefit of the doubt* instead of creating a "head-butting" situation, if you let them off the hook and are able to reach a higher place, or if you are able to take a stance of support, a calm and relaxed position, it will have a ripple effect. More people would be saying, "I can't believe how well that person handled this situation!"

You see stores that provide this type of service regularly. You see the people at Starbucks, a very well-run organization, or other brick-and-mortar stores where you walk in and are greeted immediately, and everything is pleasant, which is the experience that all customers want. Similarly, Apple stores have procedures for how their salespeople work with customers in their stores. They have a philosophy that the customer is always right, and that puts salespeople in the position to assume it is up to them to make the difference. They don't count on the customer behaving well; they just count on themselves to be excellent! If we encouraged and supported people as we went through our day, wouldn't that make the world a better place? How could that *not* affect the people around us? Wouldn't that encourage people to go to a higher place themselves? Eventually the ripple effect is very strong. It represents a very supportive position. If we all were *giving each other the benefit of the doubt*, wouldn't this world be a better place? Wouldn't everybody respond in a cool, calm, relaxed manner?

As I said, I'm 61 years old and have 7-year-old twins. I also have 38-year-old and 37-year-old sons of whom I am very proud—they are good men and great fathers. I have a granddaughter and grandson who are older than my younger kids. I look at the wonderful young men my sons are, and somehow or other they were able to accept and adapt to the point where they take the high road. My son Chris is really good at that part. People say things to him, and he just assumes the best. Every once in a while he has a little bit of a temper, but he handles things well. He has a great heart. My son Kevin is the same way. He is pretty quiet and does internalize things a lot, but he takes the same position. If you *give people the benefit of the doubt*, that will allow you to be in a better place. That will allow you to be the person who is calm and relaxed. If you *Take 10* and *hit the pause button*, it will allow you to stay calm. Situations will not raise your blood pressure.

In raising kids the second time around, one might think I would be a super-parent. Having young twins at my age—well, I wouldn't recommend it for everyone, but I can tell you it is very rewarding in a lot of ways. These kids fill me! How important it is to *take a deep breath* sometimes! Here I am writing this book about *taking 10 deep breaths* and a situation arises and I try to get into it and start breathing deeply—then halfway into it, I get interrupted!

I think I am a better person when I can pause and give people the benefit of the doubt, and I know you can do it. I encourage you to do so next time, and, as you read through this book take 10. By using the *benefit of the doubt* and the "90/10 rule," we can be a little more relaxed and accepting of the people around us. In turn, that ends up serving us, serving our neighbors, and serving our community.

We are all predisposed in how we will respond to people when we are presented with a fight-or-flight position. We could be having a horrible day. We are the homeless guy, the businessman, or somewhere in between. People will make an assessment of us, and sometimes we will be in a position when we will have to fight or flee. When we are predisposed to fight and someone comes at us, we will fight. If we are predisposed for complacency or for fleeing, then we will flee. Sometimes there is a time to stand and fight, and sometimes there is a time to turn our back and walk away. Only you know the best time for that, but you need to be in a calm, relaxed position to make the right decision.

There are some people who will tell you that there are *three options* in the fight-or-flight scenario—fight, flight, or *freeze*. At the beginning, there is a *freeze* moment when you are trying to decide what to do. I like to call that the *"pause button."* What if we consciously *hit the pause button* when we are faced with a situation like that instead of going our predisposed way? That allows us to respond to the person, and, by *hitting the pause button*, you are going to respond the way that you *want* to respond on a consistent basis—not because you are having a bad day, not because somebody just yelled at you and gave you a hard time, not because you are distant or docile and want to walk away because you've had enough.

It's been a long day, and you're tired. You have to be able to *hit the pause button*. You must respond to the situation in a calm, cool, focused way with the best information that you have. As you *hit the pause button*, you can *take 10 deep breaths*, which is about 44 seconds, and it might really help you assess the situation and approach it in the best way. Of course, you can't tell the person to give you a minute or that you need a break to breathe if they're in your face. You probably would hyperventilate, and then you wouldn't handle the situation at all—you'd just pass out! *Hit that pause button.* Step back for just a moment in your own mind, and make an assessment: What is best here? What is my best response? You are not only approaching it by understanding when somebody is in that situation, but you will also have a chance to step back and make an assessment based on what is the best way to go.

I'll see you in the next chapter. Remember, take 10, and *give that person next to you the benefit of the doubt.*

CHAPTER 2

Nothing is a greater impediment to being on good terms with others than being ill at ease with yourself.
—BALZAC

Self-Talk

There is a story about a woman who had gotten a divorce and had not dated for a long time but who had decided to finally get out into the world. She went to one of those dating sites online and found somebody she thought she would be compatible with, and they went out to dinner. About 20 minutes into the dinner, the gentleman looked over at her and said, "I see why you haven't dated for two years. You look exhausted. Your hair is a mess. The clothes you are wearing are outdated. You are way overweight. You have 'cankles,' and, quite frankly, you're not any fun to talk to, either!" With that, he folded up his napkin, put it on his plate, stood up, and walked away. It's a horrible image and something that really touches you, but here's the problem. He was never there. She wasn't out to dinner. This conversation she had was with herself. This is what she feared would happen if she tried to date, so she chose not to do so.

One of the most damaging conversations that we can have on a regular basis is not one with a boss who is overbearing, or friends who aren't supportive, or a spouse who always pushes your buttons. We all know what having that conversation feels like. Still, the most damaging conversations are the ones we have with ourselves when we are not supportive, not encouraging, when it is downright horrible! Just like the woman in the story above, these can really play with your mind. Your mind can play with your mind!

We have thoughts that echo in our minds all the time. We must try to purge the bad (negative) and put in the good (the positive). You can give people a break, give them the benefit of the doubt, but what kind of work can we do for ourselves? We need to develop a self-talk that is going to provide encouragement and help us feel supported. Those are things that we really need to work on. Retreats and meditation techniques are supposed to help us withdraw so we don't have any thoughts. Some of you have conversations going on in your mind all the time, that are just echoes of some of your abusive past. "You're stupid! You're ugly. You will never amount to anything!" All of these things just pile up on top of you. Your failure at your job. Why don't you have more money in savings? How come you're not married? Why did you get divorced? Your kids don't love you. **You** don't love you. It is constant.

If these are some of the thoughts that are haunting you, you have to understand something. First, you are not alone. I think often you have these thoughts and look at everybody else smiling or laughing and having a good time, and you think you are the only one who has these demons chasing you. In fact, there are many, many people out there who accept these curses, who have these horrible echoes in their heads. Much of this has to do with past abuses—such that you might even begin to feel like you deserved it.

Once when I was trying to deal with my abusive past, I saw Dr. Paula King, my psychologist. She asked me a question: "What would you say to the 12-year-old little boy who was standing there getting ready to get his butt kicked once again by his dad? What would you tell him?" I thought about it for a little bit and realized that what I would tell him is to fight back! To kick and scream and gouge and do whatever he can, and not to let that bastard get after him! I thought I had the right answer because by this time I was already well into my 50s. Dr. King suggested I look at the 12-year-old boy, put my arm around him, and say, "You know what? It's not your fault! It's not your fault!" A light went on in my head. I had heard that before. There was a movie years ago in which a kid had been abused. He was told it wasn't his fault, and he just started crying. I did not start crying; I probably could have because it couldn't have affected me any more. I finally realized it was not my fault.

Those thoughts that go on in your head haunt you with feelings and views that just don't make any sense. You can have these thoughts at any time. In the middle of the night you wake up and you might recall that maybe friends had said certain things to you that put doubts in your mind about yourself, about your relationships, or about your kids. Whatever the issue is, we have to love ourselves. You can go to all these seminars and talk about self-love. You can go to church, hold your hands up, and say, "Please love me." I think there are several keys we can use that will ensure we try to keep that space in our head clear.

We have to address where the thoughts come from, so the first thing you should do when you have these thoughts in your head is to pause. *Take 10 deep breaths* if you are having negative thoughts in your mind. Then start thinking to yourself, *What will this serve?* Often people will say that this is something we do to protect ourselves. We have these bad thoughts, and we dwell on worst-case scenarios so we are prepared for the worst-case scenario.

If you suspect your spouse is cheating on you and it is really hurting you in your mind, you just keep going over all these things. You want to prepare for the worst-case scenario, so you develop it in your mind and just say, "It probably is this way." With a close to 60% failure rate of marriages one way or another, she might be cheating. We all know relationships can go sour; without effective communication and connection it is easy to lose hope. Then the cycle of negative self-talk comes back to haunt you. Then you see things that aren't there because you have just beaten yourself up.

Stop! Take 10 deep breaths. There is no reason to prepare for the worst; one way or another that is not going to help you. You have to ask yourself this question: "What will it serve?" What will it serve if you keep talking to yourself and going through this over and over in your mind? It serves *nothing.*

We know that when an accident or emotional event happens, our body changes as we experience it. Our blood pressure goes up, our core temperature rises, respirations increase, and so on. Interestingly, researchers have found that when we *describe* the event later, our body responds physiologically much the same way and to the same degree it did when the accident happened. What does that tell us? You had the accident and had to go through all that stuff. Now you are telling friends about it over and over and over again. It is like an echo; it's like throwing a rock into the middle of a pond with a ripple effect. You want to tell all your friends what happened to you, explain the marks on your face, etc. It is constant.

It's the same thing with thoughts in our head. If we have bad thoughts in our head, that does affect us physiologically. Our body responds to our thinking. You wonder why you can't sleep at night? You have to clear your head! So *stop*! *Take 10 breaths*, try to relax, and ask yourself the question, "What will it serve? Am I preparing for something that is really going to make a difference, or am I just going over and over again about the same old thing—something that I can't resolve?"

It is easy to say that we need to love ourselves. Sure, sometimes we have made some bad mistakes, and it's hard to reflect back on them and think that maybe we aren't such a good person. How could I have done this or that better? Whatever the case is, you have made some poor choices along the way. Let's think about this for a bit now. You have the capacity to clear your mind, ask what will be served, and stop that conversation. So now what do you do? I have this practice that I use frequently called "radical distraction." A radical distraction is needed when you find yourself in a downward spiral when you keep beating yourself up and you need to otherwise occupy your mind. One of my favorite activities is to go to the movies. You sit there and look at the giant screen. The room is dark, filled with strangers, maybe popcorn and soda—does it get any better than that? Of course, if it is something you want to watch, that helps. I have seen some wonderful films, and having movies on DVDs these days makes it even easier and convenient to watch them. Movies take you on a journey, and, for two hours you are completely disconnected from all your thoughts and fears; you are just consumed by what is in front of you. What a wonderful journey a lot of these are! A movie can make me feel a little bit better. Is that healthy? Sometimes it is! Get away from some of the worries and concerns, and find a way to do something for yourself that is a little bit different.

Radical distractions are called that because you can just go for a run or do something else, like try a new recipe in the kitchen or hit the driving range. While that would be good for you, if you go for a run in a different area, you will be distracted. Find a way to do something that is a little bit different for yourself, so your mind is saying, "This is a different trip. All this new information is coming to me." If you are constantly in a learning position—and, as I write this book I find that happening—it is really kind of interesting to get all this new information. There is no room for a lot of self-doubt. There is no room for all these interruptions. You're too busy. You're doing all these things. You are proactive; you are really trying to take charge of your life. I truly believe that, if we can keep our mind active learning new things, we can actually reboot it, like one reboots a computer. "File wiped clean!" Let's put some new stuff in there. Are the bad thoughts still there? Yes. Is the abuse pattern still there? Yes. And you might have triggers that go off along the way—it could be a particular song; it could be somebody stirring a cocktail just before they drink it. It could be all those different things or anything that makes you say, "I remember what comes after this." At least we are not walking around with this constant specter making it difficult for us to interact.

I sometimes wonder about cell phones, the Internet, and all those different "smart" devices. I have a hard time with them sometimes because they take me away from being right in front of somebody. Eckhart Tolle talks about always being present. I see some people walking around with their cell phone, just waiting for something to happen so they can hear that familiar "ping" when they get a text. You watch the heads turn when a ping goes off and everybody thinks it's for them. I have a lot of problems with what the iPhone takes away from our interpersonal relationships, but I will say this—at least it's occupying your mind with other information as opposed to how you are talking to yourself.

Self-talk is so important to what you can do. Establish a healthy self-affirmation regimen in which you have a couple of things you are going to say to yourself each day. Think about your mind as one of your best friends who really needs constant encouragement and redirection. If you can put yourself in that position, you will have a healthier and happier day, and you will have a profound effect on people around you. Wouldn't you rather be in a positive, upbeat mood rather than either a static or negative one? A negative mood is one in which all you can do is say bad things about other people and also beat yourself up. Wouldn't it be great to just go around and encourage and help people? I know you would be a lot happier with that.

You can *take 10* during those bad thoughts and *pause for a moment* when it is happening and recognize, "Wait a minute! This isn't healthy. Why am I doing this to myself? I deserve better than this!" You can change your life by talking to yourself differently, just like you can change your relationships by speaking to others differently. Have some fun with it. A radical distraction will help you get off some of the negative messages that stream constantly, and, when you clear your mind, maybe you'll see that as a place you don't have to go. Maybe you will see people you haven't chatted with before, or maybe find a book you haven't read before. It will give you new direction.

Sometimes we can get stuck in a rut and our mind just goes to a certain place—our conditioned response when a particular event happens. Consider a journey that you take on a regular basis. You hop in your car, leave your house, and drive to work. It takes you 15 or 20 minutes to get there. You turn around and go home— same trip—over and over and over again. What happens during this journey is that, along the way (because you have taken this trip so many times), you don't even have to think about it. You take the same trip back and forth, back and forth. If this has ever happened to you—and it doesn't happen to everyone—in some cases you will forget part of the journey. You will realize you don't remember going down that road. Or you drive past something every day, and you never even see it. My wife goes into the gym every morning and walks right past a giant sauna/spa that you can win if you win a weight-loss contest. She has not seen that sign. She just goes to her pump class walking right past the sauna, back and forth. She's never seen it before. It's kind of a weird phenomenon. We are so focused on the destination that we don't remember parts of the journey.

In our minds, the same thing happens. We have this constant rhetoric that sometimes we don't even realize is being negative to ourselves. It could be that we are trying to do an extra repetition at the gym or add more weight or whatever, and we say, "Come on, you slacker! You can do it!" You are really pushing yourself, but you're using negative self-talk to do it.

The point of this chapter is that self-talk is important. You have to choose yourself, choose good thoughts for yourself, *take 10* inside your mind when you need that break, and be a better you. I hope this finds you in a good place.

Take 10, and choose you!

CHAPTER 3

One of the hardest things to do in life is
to listen without the intent to reply.
—ANONYMOUS

Listen

Wouldn't the world be a better place if we spent more time listening than talking? That quote is of special interest to me because listening more is a skill I have worked on. I wonder if you have worked on it also. You are in a conversation with a friend, and he brings up something that is very important to you. As soon as you hear the comment that piques your interest or makes you kind of sit up and listen, your mind goes to what you want to say in return. All of a sudden, you are not listening to what your friend is saying. Instead, you are preparing for either your rebuttal or your comment that confirms you believe or disbelieve what he said, some kind of contribution. It is an odd phenomenon, something that we do in marriages a lot. I really believe that if we were able to sit and listen a little bit more closely to each other, this is another step we could take. By *taking 10* when we are listening to someone, if we *pause before* responding and just appreciate what the person has to say and be present with what they are talking about, we will understand better.

There are three easy, effective ways we can become a more active listener. As I have been writing this book, I wanted a simple approach to be able to deal with life, which has gotten so out of hand that I feel we are spinning out of control. It's just going way too fast! One of the things we can do to help appreciate each other is to truly listen. I am sure that you have heard people say someone is an effective listener, or that someone else "really listens to me," or they "really hear me," they "get me," or they "understand me." What are some of the tools these good listeners employ when they are listening? Here are three easy behaviors we can use just to slow things down, hit the pause button, and make a better decision.

In a relationship, there are three ways we listen to our spouse. The first thing that happens is that he or she makes a comment, calls you by name, or says, "Hello!" The person draws your attention, and you listen to hear. Listening to hear is easy. Somebody talks, you hear them, and that's it. A noise happens in the distance, a person says, "Hey, you!" or your name is called. You may notice that, even in a crowded room, when there is a lot going on when someone says your name, you will hear your name. That is selective hearing that commands your interest—wondering what the person has to say about you or to you. This is *listening to hear.*

The next part is critical because as communication goes, we have to *see* to listen better. *Seeing to listen* is understanding people's nonverbal communication, their microexpressions. These are small expressions that people make with their faces—the way they hold their eyes, the way they turn their lips up, the way they move their eyebrows, scratch their heads, tilt their heads just a little bit—just small expressions. Another form of nonverbal communication is to look at someone's whole body as they are talking. Notice how their feet point to you, how they hold their hands, if they lean forward or sit back. *Seeing to listen* is a very good way of understanding where a person is coming from and also really connecting with them. If you are not looking at people when they talk, you may be missing a lot of what they are saying.

Nonverbal communication makes up around 70% to 75% of the meaning of a conversation. Words are 30% or less, with part of that being how a speaker uses his voice. That's why texting is so challenging. If you get a text, you don't get to hear their voice. You don't get to see what they look like when they're saying it. You miss so much in that text. Texting has to be one of the least-communicative ways of communicating.

You *listen to hear*, and you *listen to understand*. The third one is *listening to feel*. When you are truly connected to someone, you *listen to feel*. What is that like? You understand they are having a good day or a bad day. You understand how they feel about this particular subject—maybe they are very passionate about it. It could be they are indifferent. It doesn't make any difference—you understand how they feel. You are truly connected to that person if you *listen to feel*. You *hit the pause button* and you *count to 10*. When you are listening to someone, of course you must count in your head, or you cannot be listening well. Pause before you say anything to them, and just let them finish talking. *Push the pause button on your response*, on what you are thinking, and just listen. Just consume what they have to say. Drink it in. Appreciate it! Feel where they are coming from.

How do we know this works? Have you ever heard a couple when they have just begun dating? The woman will say something like, "He is so amazing! It's like he can read my mind!" When you are first dating, what is happening? You are listening. You are zeroed in. You have singular vision on your partner's eyes—you are taking it all in! You also feel where your partner is coming from. If this person is passionate about horses and talking about them and you're watching him talk about horses, you can feel how it would be to ride a horse, to feel the interaction with this animal. You're right there with your partner because you are so connected.

How do we know when it doesn't work? Years later, when the couple is in a counseling office and trying to save their marriage because they have grown apart, one of the things either the wife or husband will say to the counselor is, "He doesn't hear me," or "She doesn't listen to me," and "We don't talk anymore." "Yes, we talk all the time, but you don't hear me!" What has happened is that, as we have grown accustomed to one another, we quit paying as much attention. Perhaps the husband is watching ESPN. There is no way he can singularly focus on his wife when she is talking because he is doing other things—eating, watching a game, tending to the kids. We are doing all these things we have to do over the course of a day. Our lives are busy. We have to get it done, but isn't that something? We no longer really hear our significant other.

My wife will make a comment, and I will say, "Yeah." I actually default to "Yes" every time she says something. "Honey, blah blah blah." "Yup!" I don't even know what she said. It is a default response. A lot of people say "Yes" or "No" automatically. It might be interesting to do a study to see what personality type responds automatically "Yes" (optimists?) and which responds automatically "No" (pessimists?).

However, when my wife tells me I wasn't listening, and I respond that I was, she will invariably ask me, "Well, what did I just say?" It's like the dreaded "Pop Quiz" in college. I sit there, befuddled, thinking, *Oh, no! I didn't take notes. I'm not ready!*

To truly stay connected, we have to master these three types of listening. Many people talk about the art of listening, and many very smart, very highly acclaimed authors have written books on the subject, have made terrific presentations. What I want to do is bring it down to its purist, simplest form. When somebody is talking to you, listen to them, look at them, and feel their passion. *Take 10 seconds* to really hear them. *Pause and put everything on hold* that you are thinking. Stay truly connected. Listen to what they have to say. Believe me, you are going to get gems that are just amazing.

We have so much to offer each other. Whether you're a doctor or a janitor or a business owner or a guy who drives cars for a living—we are all amazing, incredible, beautiful human beings. If we took the time to listen to what each other has to say, I think we would be amazed.

Coming up in the next chapter, we will see something that is unique inside all of us—unique because it is a gift. Right now, just *hit the pause button. Take 10* and *really be present when somebody is talking to you.* Put down your cell phone. Look into their eyes, watch their faces. Truly listen to stay connected. *Listen to hear, see to listen, and listen to feel.*

Take 10 deep breaths, and truly listen.

CHAPTER 4

Genius is in you, but like a seed, you
determine whether it dies or grows.
—MOTS HONA DHELI WAYO

Your Genius Gift

As I write this chapter, I am sitting in a bed-and-breakfast in Ouray, Colorado. I look around, and I see that the owners have paid close attention to detail. The wallpaper is nearly seamless in the way it is lined up, and the fit and finish and the way each part is designed shows such attention to detail that it is amazing to me. Someone really took the time to make this a cool place to be. From the lamps, to the bed, every aspect of it: it is built for comfort, built for people on a little minivacation like we are.

Once, when I was about 12 years old, I was watching a man across the street in the neighborhood where I grew up. He was putting stucco on a house. In one movement, he would scoop the material out of the bucket, put it onto the house, put his scoop back into the bucket, and then back onto the house. In a way, it was almost like he was conducting an orchestra. His movement was so fluid and natural that it looked effortless. Ever since then, I have noticed people when they were doing something that seemed natural to them.

An example of the *genius gift* in sports is the phenomenon called "being in the zone." On February 2, 2009, in Madison Square Garden, Kobe Bryant "dropped 61" against the Knicks. He was 20 for 20 at the free-throw line, and he was so focused that he said nothing after the game. For Bryant not to talk was really amazing. He was still "in the zone." Another example is "The Immaculate Reception." On December 23, 1972, Franco Harris grabbed a ball out of the air. He was in the zone! It is 45 years later, and this catch is still remembered. Then, in 1981, there was "The Catch," so named because Joe Montana of the 49ers threw a faultless pass that was perfectly caught by Dwight Clark in the NFC championship game, with 58 seconds left in the game. This was an instance when there were actually *two* people in the zone. Professional sports is full of examples of people's *genius gifts*. So is art—buildings, paintings, photography—all creative and natural to the person bringing it to life.

But what about everyone else—all the ordinary people? What is it that is inside us that propels us forward to do what we do as well as we can? Sometimes if we are working outside of what we do naturally, then we do a job that isn't perfect, and it feels cumbersome and overwhelming. Wayne Dyer, whom the world lost a few years back, was an extremely inspirational and encouraging man to me and many others. He constantly said, "Find your passion! Follow your passion, and the universe will take care of you."

As an example, the universe is some giant cash machine in the sky, and if you are doing something you are supposed to be doing, money will rain down on you? I don't think so. Is money the end-all? Well, you have to pay your bills and such, but what is the phenomenon that happens when you are working within your passion? What is it that goes on? What is that *genius gift* inside you? I believe that everyone has a *genius gift* inside them. It could be writing; it could be talking; it could be socializing. It could be cooking the perfect meal or nurturing your family in other ways. It could be many different things.

The *genius gift* is different in everybody. In particular, your *genius gift* is yours alone, and you know when you are operating within its scope. How do you know that? Because whatever you are doing, there's never enough time to do it. It comes completely natural, you feel so comfortable doing it, and it's also beneficial to you and to others. You are very productive when you are in that realm.

How do we know what the *genius gift* looks like in action? Consider the man who cleans the bank and really takes pride in doing so. Potentially, that is his gift. He knows exactly how to clean the bank in the most efficient way and in the least amount of time. Maybe he is listening to music—that is his escape—as he cleans the stairway and the floors, as he does everything in a systematic way so as to be most efficient and effective. He is in the zone, using his gift. He finishes at the end of the night and surveys his "product," the clean bank. He looks back with great satisfaction, much like a construction worker who builds a home, the architect who designs it, or the people who decorate it. Each of them has a *genius gift* and hopefully is working within his passion.

As we work within our passion, it has an amazing effect. What happens? Consider the person who cleans the bank as opposed to the president who runs the bank or the CEO—what's the difference between the two? The CEO of the bank's *genius gift* is working with numbers. He looks at numbers, and they are organic to him. They come alive, and he arranges them. The gentleman who cleans the bank makes sure it is clean so people will come to the bank and do business. They both operate within their gifts. And as they do, they each have information for the other that could be very helpful.

As the janitor is working within his gift, he could go talk to the CEO of the bank and say, "I have a way that could save you thousands of dollars if you only took these few steps." The banker says, "I have a way that could help you save thousands of dollars per year and put it away for your children and for your comfort and for you to travel."

People don't necessarily know more than us, and they don't always know less than us. They just know different! They are not better, and they are not less; they are just different! If we can level the playing field and recognize that each one of us has a *genius gift* inside, we could appreciate each other so much more. We could see others' gifts.

At the bed-and-breakfast where we stayed, the woman who made our breakfast was also the owner. We complimented her on how wonderful the surroundings were, how good the breakfast tasted, and said the whole presentation was amazing. As we spoke about it with her, we could see that she lit up. This was something she was passionate about. Her *genius gift* may be taking care of people. It could be that this is her passion and she follows it because it is rewarding to her. It is not only paying the bills; it is also helping build a nest egg for her and her family.

Isn't it fun when we watch somebody in the zone? Isn't it fun when we watch somebody utilizing their *genius gift*? What happens when we are outside that? First, we have to remember again that everyone has one. How do you find yours? What is it that you are truly passionate about? What is something that really gets your attention and when you talk about it, you are more animated? Your hands are up! Your eyes are lit! You just feel the energy coursing through your body; you can feel, "This is something that excites me!"

How do we know when we are in that zone? You can just watch yourself or have other people tell you what they think you are really interested in. They will know! Close friends will know what you are passionate about because when you talk about it, you change. You can feel yourself change, but sometimes you cannot see it, so ask somebody else.

Chapter 4: Your Genius Gift

Why is it that when you are operating outside your *genius gift*, you get dragged down and overwhelmed? You have to pay the bills, but how do you feel working only for that goal? You must strive to find your *genius gift* and know exactly what it is. Know that it's there. Realize that you have it inside, and figure out how to use it. Of course, I'm going to tell you that you have to *take 10* to find it. *Take 10 deep breaths, take 10 steps, or take 10 seconds* to just think of what is inside of you that really motivates you. What is inside that you are really passionate about? Of course you're passionate about your family, your wife, your extended family, your children, and so on, but what is it that makes you happy to get out of bed in the morning? When do you put your hands on something and realize, "Yes, this is my *genius gift*! I am operating in that zone." Then compare it to your current job. Being a sales manager for 30 years, my task was to sell cars. My task was to help get good salespeople to come work for me and to help them sell cars. I used to say all that time, "I'm not really that good a manager. I'm just a really good salesperson."

I love to open people's minds so they can see that they have incredible gifts. I love to introduce people to their special gift. I love to be able to look at it and say, "Wow! You're really something!" (Side note: if you give a compliment, make sure it is appropriate, but also make sure it is sincere. Don't walk up to a beautiful girl and say, "Wow! You're so beautiful!" It's just not appropriate. And, if you're insincere, the person will see that you're just giving a compliment to see if you can get him or her to do something. Measure those compliments, and measure how you encourage people by that one thing.)

Evaluate your current job. What is it that you're doing? Compare it to what you believe is your *genius gift*. Using myself as an example, for 30 years I have been managing people in the car business, yet my passion is to encourage and help people. My passion has always been to help people find their *genius gift* within, but, at the end of the day, my goal was to sell cars. Things got muddled between the two. If I had inserted my *genius gift* into my job and used encouragement, direction, and helping people find their own *genius gifts*, I could have been even more successful than I was. By many measures I was successful. In a lot of ways I did help people; I did encourage others. Because there was an agenda involved (and sometimes it seemed less than sincere), it was hard for people to perceive, and I was sometimes misunderstood. My encouragement, direction, and support for searching out their *genius gifts* were misperceived as me trying to talk them into buying or selling a car.

Chapter 4: Your Genius Gift

What happens if we take our *genius gift* and put it inside a job? If we are working at a job that is within our *genius gift*, the days just sail by. I am not suggesting that work should be effortless, but when it is fun, it may seem easier, and time goes by more quickly. I would encourage you to do a little work on your *genius gift* each day. That will reward you and help you feel fulfilled. Do it at a certain time each day (maybe the hour driving to work or back home); do something or listen to something that touches your *genius gift*. Take steps to find ways to work within your *genius gift*. Educate yourself. Put yourself in a position—financially, geographically, or whatever the case may be—to explore your *genius gift*.

Let's find a way to connect you with your *genius gift*. How do you know what it is? It's when you're *in that zone*. It's effortless; it's seamless; it's amazing. How do we get to it? You *take 10*, *hit the pause button*, and look inside or think about some of the things you do that really help you through the day. This is something that can really help us sustain that wonderful life we are looking for. So *take 10 deep breaths*. Consider this chapter and think about it. Look inside you. What *is* my *genius gift*? How can I make it work—either for my current job or in another career?

I encourage people to read *Discover Your Strengths* by Donald Clifton and Sally Byrne Woodbridge. This book encourages people to know and work on their strengths. Often we work so hard on our weaknesses and trying to improve those aspects of ourselves that we get discouraged. Spend more time working on your strengths, because in your strengths somewhere is your *genius gift*. Think about how that would work for you. Focus on your strengths. You still have to work on your weaknesses, but spend less time on your weaknesses and more time on your strengths. That will invigorate you. That will make you feel more excited and also will help you work on your weaknesses.

Take 10 deep breaths—look within and find your *genius gift*.

CHAPTER 5

*We must begin where we are and move
forward immediately by starting small
and capitalizing on what's at hand.*
—MIKE SCHMOKER

The Snap-Back Effect

At my size, somewhere around 6 feet 8 inches tall and around 300 pounds (give or take 20 pounds), I have gained and lost probably 300 pounds. I could basically be at zero. I don't know if that makes any sense or not, but "the snap-back effect" is something that I have thought about after seeing people go through radical changes. Say you go on a diet and lose all the weight you need to. You do a really good job. You're focused. You're driven. In my case, I went all the way down from 318 pounds to 273 pounds. I lost pants sizes along the way, had them altered, and then not only gained the weight back but additional poundage as well. I lost about 45 pounds; then I regained those 45 pounds and also added to them. As is the case with most of these chapters, this is a subject I have thought about for a long time. As you age, I guess you just mull things over in your mind longer.

I don't know if I have come up with any better answers. Like Socrates taught, maybe you just come up with really good questions. There is a question I kept asking myself: "How is it that we can make these radical changes but cannot maintain them?" The snap-back effect is what happens when you get to a point past where you've ever been before and then snap back to where you were or, worse yet, to a state worse than where you started.

Years ago, I went to a Tony Robbins seminar. He is arguably one of the best motivational speakers there is. The seminar was two and a half days long at the beautiful Broadmoor Hotel in downtown Colorado Springs. All the 2700 people were in a big auditorium. We were supposed to do fire-walking, which I hoped was just a metaphor but turned out to be the real deal. I had seen people do it, but I thought there had to be a trick to it; ordinary people cannot walk on live coals like that! Sure enough, it was no trick, and we did walk on fiery coals. How we did it, I have no idea, but I can tell you this—almost everybody who went and participated ended up walking on fire, at least 2600 out of 2700 people! That's a remarkable thing!

Participants listened through all the talks, got the workbooks and books—how to lose weight, how to be a better husband and father, and all these wonderful things. People left with a wealth of information and all kinds of great ideas on how to change their lives. I came back and was pretty inspired. My wife, April, looked at me like, "Who is this guy?" I was on fire! I wanted to change the world! I wanted to change my neighbors, change myself first, of course, but I was so inspired and so excited. I wanted to meditate *now*! Hurry up to meditate now! Change this or change that! As I said earlier, I'm not good at meditating—five minutes into it and I'm asleep. Even in the most awkward positions, I can fall asleep. That's probably why I am writing this at 4:00 a.m.

Here's an amazing thing! Five people from my city went to this seminar. Five people returned, fully charged, ready to come back and make a difference in our community. All of us got to a point after a while where it not only faded, but it also caused problems. I am aware that two of the women who went with us ended up with problems in their marriages. A gentleman who accompanied me, whom I knew from the place I worked, for him not only did it not take and stick with him, but he became worse. He had been a somewhat angry person. I'm not meaning to be unkind by saying that, but he just had a very serious, angry way about him. He went back to that mood and personality within just a couple of weeks. Isn't that something?

During certain evangelical crusades, people come forward, having made a life-changing decision. All these people come forward, yet follow-up measuring the success rate reveals that five years later, around 85% to 90% of them had returned to their original lifestyle *or worse*. The or *"worse"* part is the thing that is disturbing. If they had stayed in the mode they were and had not gone forward in that altar call, they might feel a little bit better. Now, not only did they go to all the way back to where they had been, but they become less than that. What does that say about "lifestyle change?" Dieters may eat more and more of the wrong stuff. Anyone can return to making poor decisions. It is challenging to maintain!

As I referenced before, the movie called *What About Bob?* with Richard Dreyfuss and Bill Murray showcases them at their best. It was a hilarious movie about a gentleman (Bill Murray) with obsessive-compulsive disorder. In the movie, Richard Dreyfuss's character had written a book called *Baby Steps*. Believe me, the message of this movie was not lost on me. We all might be able to pick up a tip from a movie or book or watching someone else and make ourselves feel a little bit better about ourselves or perhaps gain the motivation to change things. In the book *Baby Steps*, the challenge was to take small steps.

We cannot make radical changes in our lives and maintain them without the external stimuli changing radically around us. If we're going to make these big changes in our lives and expect them to hold, we are going to have to be surrounded by people and circumstances to help us hold onto those changes—people who agree with and appreciate our change. Or we can choose not to hang around with people who might discourage us or disparage our attempts to better ourselves. I think it is really encouraging to see some people when they lose the weight (and I go to the gym every day and see them) and they keep it off—that's always inspiring to me. I am always appreciative of their dedication and their drive.

What are some of the steps we can take to maintain our changes? First, the title of the book, *Take 10*, is to encourage people to take time, help them be patient, not to rush things. *Hitting the pause button* helps you avoid knee-jerk reactions. Don't make rash decisions or act too quickly. The driving force for me in writing this book is that I observe things around me. I hear things around me. I watch the news (probably too much), and I see people always in such a hurry—to go where? If we could slow down and have a little more patience in our lives with ourselves and with each other, that would be a powerful and important thing for us. If we take small, calculated steps as opposed to a severe redirect to get to a particular place, it could help us sustain our accomplishment.

Say we need to quit drinking alcohol (and I know it is highly addictive, just like smoking and drugs), a simple first step might be to drink less or not have liquor available around you, but you also have to avoid places where people drink. This is adjusting the external stimuli that affect your desire to drink. Same thing with smoking cigarettes: you would have to quit entirely and then avoid places where there are people who smoke. Not keeping cigarettes around and avoiding smokers involve changing external stimuli.

What more can we do? We have to change our mindset, so we have to take 10 and *hit the pause button*. We have to look at what our path is, set a goal for where we want it to lead, and do so in a very calm, calculated way. I have been in several weight-loss programs and contests. I like working out—but I do get a little careless sometimes with my eating. I could easily weigh 400 pounds if I just totally let myself go. There is such good food available! You can't tell me that a hot buttered cinnamon roll is not good stuff! It really is, but is it good *for* you? Probably not. If you take that away and put an apple in its place, it won't be quite the same, but it will take you one step closer to your goal. It's okay to splurge once in a while, but one can't be healthy without consuming healthy foods and avoiding unhealthy ones. Garbage in, garbage on!

Taking smaller steps is important. They will keep us from becoming overwhelmed by our decisions and goals. The only way to maintain your drive and the intensity of change is to use a balanced attack. You must avoid bad stimuli and seek out good stimuli in order to be balanced and move forward. In the dieting example, to lose weight we would need to eat less while making choices to eat healthier foods. We would have to exercise more and drink more water instead of juice or pop. All these steps, each of which is small and calculated, as opposed to a radical change, keep us going in the right direction.

Occasionally—and unfortunately—crisis situations do arise. They may be life-changing, and a person or family has no control over them—they may even be self-induced. They may be so critical that changes have to be made *now*, or the events might alter the very core of the person involved. Intervention, oversight, and professional help should be sought. With the proper guidance, I have seen wonderful turns of events showing the true nature of the human spirit and our ability to adapt to adversity. Life will give us an opportunity to reboot ourselves.

We are such a conditioned group. We're all acquainted with Pavlov's dog, which began salivating at the sound of a bell after having been fed for days after a bell was rung. If we open the refrigerator or the cupboard, maybe we begin salivating or have a sense of "appetite." We are conditioned to respond to external stimuli on a regular basis. If you see a red light, you'd better stop. If you see a green light, you can go. If you hear a little pinging sound indicating you received a text, you really want to check your phone (and everybody around you does, too). I have heard that you cannot condition everyone to respond to a bell, yet here we are responding. I always thought it was ironic that smart phones use a bell-like sound—the "ping"—for text notification. Maybe some future generation of smart phones will be personalized to say your name. "Hey, Kevin, you've got a text!"

That is the key to the snap-back effect. You have to change the external stimuli in your life, you have to change some of the conditions around you, and you have to do it in moderation and over time. Any severe course change is going to create a severe snap-back effect.

I have been amazed by some of the successes people have achieved, but I have seen more failures than successes. That is unfortunate; I wish I could have seen more successes.

I don't think success happens because one person is stronger than another. People are just different and take different approaches to their problems. If we are a little more relaxed, a little calmer, if we *take 10* and make sure that we are calculating and not rushing the course adjustment, we have a great chance to maintain what we hope to achieve. We have a chance to succeed.

There are success stories. It's not like there aren't abundant examples of people who can hold on to change. There *are* people who can do that. There are people who go about losing weight at just two pounds a week. They go about changing their lifestyle a little at a time. Being patient is one of the things about *Take 10* that we really have to embrace. We have to realize that *we must pause.* We must embrace the fact that sometimes we must just *be quiet, be patient, be peaceful, and take 10. Take 10 and avoid the snap-back effect!*

CHAPTER 6

To a brave man, good luck and bad luck are
like his left and right hands. He uses both.
—St. Catherine of Siena

Bravery in Leadership

I promised that the last seven chapters of the book would be based on "BE GREAT!" This is an acronym for bravery in leadership, encouragement, gratitude, respect, empathy, adaptability to adversity, time and trust. When I was nearly finished writing the book, I realized there was a lot more to be shared so I added some more thoughts.

Bravery in leadership is something for which we have examples throughout history. Often we see people who are leaders in commerce, industry, the military, the government, or some other position of power. True leadership can be shown in the smallest and least noticed of positions. Not being a leader does not mean that you are weak, "only" a follower. People who follow are not weak. People who follow are just not clear on which direction to take, so they follow a leader, a person who is very clear on which way to go. A perfect example is iPhone's Siri. I don't know how I got anywhere before without our little friend on the phone. I ask her for directions, I tell her the address where I need to go, and she takes me all the way up to the doorstep. In the past, the biggest problem with maps for me was how to fold the darned thing up so I could put it away. Some of you may never have had that problem, but believe me, that was one of my issues with maps. I could not put one back together the way it was supposed to be. My whole glove-box would be filled with just one map, all unfurled and crammed in there, just because I couldn't fold it right.

This ability to get somewhere easily is amazing to me! My wife thinks I am directionally challenged or have a hard time with directions. I tell her the good news is that everywhere I was going, I got there! I always got where I needed to go, or else I wouldn't be here.

Siri is a leader. She tells you exactly where to go and how to get there. She very politely tells you to redirect if you make a wrong turn. *"Take a left, then take another left. Stay the course!"* We hear that voice, and we know it is mechanical or however they do that. We know there is not some lady sitting in a basement somewhere giving directions on the phone. I think it would be a great prank to have someone live stand in for Siri. At any rate, Siri is a leader because she gives us directions

I have experienced great leaders in my time. Throughout my working life I have experienced some amazing leaders—very encouraging, very loving, very supportive. The people who worked for them were very dear to these people.

I was blessed to be able to work in the Bureau of Prisons at the U.S. Prison at Lompoc (a federal penitentiary). I noticed that other corrections officers would talk about their time on the job as "being in there" like the prisoners. When an officer walks into general population, he can't just turn and walk back out. The men and women who do these jobs deserve our great respect and appreciation. I was able to join that group for a short time, and I can tell you that it was no easy job. Leaders among the corrections officers were those who took action. There were some of us who were new to the job. One "Operations Lieutenant," Lieutenant Young, had been an Army Ranger. He was in phenomenal shape and exuded being in charge. He was just an amazing man. As a leader, whenever there was a skirmish or a problem in the prison, he would take the lead, and everyone else would feel more comfortable.

In one particular situation, I was in one of the units, and a fight broke out. I was kind of in the mix of it. I had my situation contained for the most part, but Lieutenant Young showed up as backup, put his hand on my shoulder, and said, "Barclay, how are you doing?" Knowing he was there behind me made me feel comfortable. He was leading from behind. He saw how I responded and was appreciative. You don't have too many chances for mistakes or poor judgment while working in the prison because you are dealing with people who have made such poor choices in their lives that sometimes they have little to lose.

One of my job assignments was to "walk the steam line." I didn't know what they were talking about, so I followed another corrections officer through the corridors of the prison to get to the front of the dining common area. There was the steam line, with vegetables, the meat of the day, etc. My job (after going through training at the academy for six weeks at Glynco, Georgia), and feeling pretty good about myself and ready to go, was to make sure that everybody got only two cookies. The prisoners came up, and all of them were grabbing cookies. I said, "Two cookies, two cookies." I had to stop some guys. One guy grabbed a handful of cookies, and I said, "Two cookies!" He looked at me and then slammed those cookies on top of the metal sneeze guard over the food. He pushed the crumbs around and said to me, "What do you think about that?" During the training at the academy, we learned that the dining commons is one of the more dangerous areas because they have utensils available that could be used as weapons. We were to be on our guard. I thought to myself that I hadn't been doing this very long, and here I was, about to start a riot in the prison because of cookies. That was a horrible situation! It's interesting how your body responds to a crisis. From the waist up, I felt like I was pretty calm, because I knew what was happening—it was a test. He was looking at me, waiting for my response. The inmates on either side of him were looking at him, then looking at me, and I was thinking to myself, *What am I doing here?!* The bottom part of my body wanted to run away. I remember distinctly, because I had safety boots on, that my heel was tapping when I was standing up. I remember not really thinking but just saying, "It looks like you get no dessert." That tickled him. He looked at me, and one of the other guys actually smirked. Then they went on their way. One of the cooks on the line told me I had handled it great. All I had said was the obvious. He doesn't get his cookies, so he doesn't get dessert! It wasn't some genius play; it was just stating the obvious because I didn't know what else to say.

I handled that situation as a leader, and people looked at me and thought I had handled it well. I was definitely an "accidental" leader in this situation! Afterwards I was told how good a job I had done in what could have been an explosive confrontation. I actually had some of the inmates look at me differently from then on, and that was pretty good.

I remember taking that job because I wanted to challenge myself. I was getting out of the car business and into something else, and I wanted to challenge myself to see if I could do something like that. I was always a big guy, with plenty of challenges along the way, as you have read already. I wanted to be known as brave, courageous. I wanted to be known as a leader. I have always been put in that position because of my size. I remember people in the neighborhood where I grew up saying to their kids, "If Kevin Barclay is going to go, you can go." In college, I remember the coach saying one time, "Hey, if you want something done, ask Kevin Barclay."

We see challenging things as leaders. I think it is really important for us to know that we all have that opportunity and ability to lead. Whether we are in the front of the band or in the back of the bus, we can lead.

So what does bravery in leadership look like? How can we be brave leaders? How can we be courageous in leading others? How can we be outstanding in leading ourselves and our families? I think part of it is just *assuming the role*. I believe as leaders in our communities, or in our households, we have to just accept the fact that this is our job. "This is what I'm going to do. I'm going to lead my family." "I'm going to lead my business." "I'm going to lead the people around me." Once we assume that role, it takes on a whole new direction, a new feeling. We have to recognize that people are counting on us to make the right decision. Just like Siri. We are counting on her to give us the best directions. People who run a business have people who work for them counting on them to make the right decisions. Just like your family— they are counting on you to make the right decisions. We have to look at things and *pause, take 10*, and 10 is not a long time. A 10-second period of time can be over very quickly. If you rush through it, *taking 10* could be 1-2-3-4-5-6-7-8-9-10, and you're done in about three seconds. On the other hand, *taking 10* can be a lifetime.

As we *pause* and look at the direction we are going in, sometimes there is no choice. When you are a prison guard, you do not have time to pause. You have to react; it is a job of reacting. Police *have* to react: something happens, and they show up. Firefighters *have* to react. God bless the people in those positions! The men and women who do those jobs are heroes! You are *reacting* to an unknown situation—you don't necessarily know what came before or what is going to happen next. Someone needs help *now*. Sometimes we do not have time to pause, but in leadership of businesses or leadership of our families, we *do* have the time to just *take a moment and evaluate* whether this is the right decision for my family, my business, my friends.

As leaders, we have to be patient and calculating. Sometimes we have to do things quickly, but more often than not, we can make informed decisions. There will be calculations. We say, "Siri, we have to go here," and she already knows how to get there. We look at our team and say, "We have to go here. This is how we are going to get there." Then they follow us.

After 30 years in management in the car business, I realize now that I was often an ineffective leader. I look back at those times and remember saying to more than a handful of people around me that maybe I wasn't a good manager. Maybe I'm just an exceptional salesperson. One of the things leaders do is to surround themselves with effective people and allow them to do their jobs. One of the ineffective things I was doing as a leader in that business was *doing my employees' jobs for them—enabling* them. I couldn't fault them. If someone else is going to do the work, why wouldn't they let him? I enjoyed the process so much, I would go ahead and take it away from them, and I would just do it. I didn't try to take credit for it, and that is part of leadership too, but I was looking to get it done. Effective, brave leaders allow their people to do their work and expect their people to do their best work. They lead them in such a way that their people can do better. The leader does not step up and do their work unless it is a dire situation.

Brave leaders will step up and say, "You know what? Let's go side by side on this, and you can see how I would handle it, and then we will move forward." That is how people grow. They grow by being able to do a job. They grow in confidence and in ability when they are led. I made a mistake when I would take over if a salesperson came to me and said, "I'm not going to be able to make this deal." I should have said, "Of course you can! Go back and try this or that." I sometimes tried that, and they did not seem reassured, so then I said, "Okay, give me the stuff. I'll go deal with it."

A brave and effective leader *leads*; an effective leader does not *do*. The mistake I made was thinking I was doing the right thing. Rather than encouraging salespeople and coaching them, I would just grab it and make the sale. I sold lots of cars that way, but the people around me felt that I was doing it to get attention. The people around me misunderstood my intentions as a leader. I was just doing it so they could have the sale. Then I looked at the results and thought, "What happened?"

Lieutenant Young was fantastic. He would send people out and tell them, "Get this done!" He would expect results. People in the military know how things work. Depending on what rank you are, you tell the people below your rank to get something done, and they go get it done! You expect it. If the results are not what you wanted, then you must talk with them. It is amazing to see how that works. Effective leaders in business make assignments and then step away. I was an incredible salesman and accomplished a lot of things in my automotive career, but there were other things I could have done a little bit differently to help others become great salespeople, too. Knowing what I know now, I know exactly what a brave leader is *not*.

The next part of brave leadership is realizing that to identify what something is, you have to identify what it is *not*. Brave leadership does not jump in and do the work or the task for someone else or assume the task for somebody. That is not being a leader. Being a brave, intentional leader is directing and encouraging people to do the right thing. I found one person I worked with challenging in a lot of ways. We had some things against us to begin with, but it was challenging, I can tell you. Looking at him as a leader and watching him rise through the ranks, it was obvious to me what a courageous leader is *not*. One of the things a courageous leader does not do is take credit for what other people have done or take credit for other people's ideas. I always try to give people the *benefit of the doubt* (remember the first chapter) and think their intentions are pure. There has to be something in there—some good intentions somewhere—so I make the mistake of assuming that is where people are starting. I still am incredibly surprised when I find out that is not the case.

Courageous leaders are not jealous. Brave leaders are good leaders, and they recognize the talents of others and embrace them. They encourage them. Looking back at 20 years in my community, I have been blessed to participate in a lot of wonderful fundraisers and support community activities: the American Red Cross, American Diabetes Association, Suicide Foundation (locally) were all groups I felt strongly about. I produced and directed shows for each one of those as fundraisers that went very well. I was very proud to be part of those. A courageous leader will embrace and support the community efforts of their team. I would admonish and encourage you right now to remember that if you are a leader, you have individuals who work with you or work for you and who are counting on you (and I always have such a hard time saying "work *for*," because I believe people should be working as a team). One of my mentors, Mike F., always introduced me as somebody he worked *with*, and we will talk about him a little bit later.

Courageous leaders do not discourage participation in community events. They accept and encourage it because they know it makes not only them look better but makes the business look better. I was ridiculed and second-guessed and made a fool of for doing these things. The impression of some people around me was that I wanted to be on stage and in front of people, adored, and appreciated. Well, first of all, let me say as a side note—who *doesn't* want to be adored and appreciated? If you can't admit that, then at least try to understand it. It's not like we want to be hated and reviled, right? We don't get up in the morning saying, "I want to be hated and reviled today. As a leader of our business, I want people to hate me, so I'm going to act in such a way as to make that happen." Sometimes I wonder. I see people who are leaders and wonder if they had that little talk with themselves in the morning. Brave and courageous leaders don't do that.

Brave and courageous leaders do not jump to conclusions or assume that other people have agendas. They expect the best of other people, because when you do that, you will get that more often than not. Sometimes you expect the best, and you get surprised. That's tough! I get it. You expect the best, and you think those who follow you are really going to give their best to you, and then they don't. Courageous leaders do not second-guess other people's agendas. They encourage and embrace their direction. Being a brave and courageous leader is challenging. Often people will unexpectedly jump to the lead. I can remember instances from both my corrections-officer experience and my business life when people said, "I can do that." I applaud and appreciate all the people who do that. Taking on a leadership role naturally is an amazing thing to see.

Make sure you check with the man in the mirror. Make sure you are the person who can lead. Don't assume a role because of something you want. Assume the role because it is something you know you can do. Being a leader is nothing to take for granted. It's not something to be flippant about. If you're in the lead, you take charge, you get stuff done, and you allow other people to get stuff done. You empower them, support them. It's sad that I had to learn about all these things at the end of my career; I could have used them earlier. I still was successful in a lot of ways in the car business, and many positives came out of it. If you examine yourself on a daily basis and discover different ways to do something, then do them—you will be better for it. Don't wait until the end of your career to learn this; do it now! Embrace this idea. Allow your people to do their jobs. Expect, train, and encourage. Really allow people to *shine*.

I was able to write this book only because I had two great mentors in my business career: Mike F. and Gary V., who was also a great leader to me and a great mentor. The single best characteristic in both of them was that they wanted me to be the best I could be and allowed me the freedom to become that. They appreciated my unique personality as well. I'm outgoing and truly love people. Sometimes that is hard for others to recognize. Of all the people who have worked alongside me on my journey, those two gentlemen really helped to make me a better man, and to them, I say, "Thank you!"

Being a courageous leader is not an easy job. If it were, there would be a big long line of people waiting to do it. Whether we are leading one person, a hundred people, or a thousand people, whether we are leading a country or just leading ourselves, we need to be brave in our leadership. We need courage, direction, and resolve. We need to embrace those we are leading. Don't discourage them—encourage them. Don't dwell on their weaknesses; help them through their problems and point out their successes. If you are called to lead, you are called to be exceptional. Don't take yourself too seriously, however. Take the job seriously, take the position seriously, take your tasks seriously, but stay humble. You are not "all that." Bravery in leadership means being vulnerable. Bravery in leadership is understanding your own faults, not just those of the people around you. Bravery in leadership is doing things to allow those around you to be exceptional.

Bravery in leadership requires patience as well. Wise decision-making requires thought as well as courage. I admonish, encourage, and appreciate you being a leader. Not all of us can do it.

I want to encourage you to *take 10* and be a courageous leader.

CHAPTER 7

He who encourages others, dignifies himself.
—A CHINESE PROVERB

Encouragement

What does encouraging other people say about that person? Encouraging or reaching out to others is an indication that the person is sincere. They offer help without an agenda—just to be helpful. We know an encouraging word is sincere when we say it. Because it is heartfelt, we feel love for that person. We just want to reach out and connect. It fulfills a need in us to socialize and stay connected to people. Our current obsession with social media gives us a false sense of being connected, but it is empty. We know that nonverbal communication is a large part of listening and learning about others—it is, at very least, about 60%. When somebody is talking to you, they say more than the mere words they are using. We must also pay attention to how they are using the words, how they are looking at you, and how they move.

Nonverbal communication is important because it is controlled by our subconscious. We don't *consciously* decide to lift our hands and point at somebody. We don't *consciously* look to the left, which is often the sign of a falsehood. Our subconscious controls our nonverbal communications; that is what makes them so real!

Understanding that and realizing that nonverbal aspects are such a big part of communication, face-to-face communication is still the most important kind of communication there can be. If we are communicating only via texts or email, then we are not getting the full picture. We are not fully communicating. Even telephone conversation is better than digital—it at least allows us to hear a voice and maybe subtle nuances in tone, revealing emphasis. When an encouraging word comes out and is sincere, people can feel it. If it is insincere, they can feel it as well. When it is time to give an encouraging word to somebody, *pause and take 10*. Reflect on what you're about to say so you can say the thing most needed at that moment. Measure what you are about to say as to your sincerity. Do you have an agenda attached to the praise? Are you trying to win their favor? Are you trying to push them to do things your way? When you see a good man doing a good thing, you should want to encourage him to continue. You should want to shake his hand and wish him well. Encouraging remarks must be appropriate—spoken both at an appropriate time and in an appropriate manner. Just yesterday I had a great conversation with a doctor in town who had had a horrific bicycle accident. He is back at the gym already and battling through recovery. It is remarkable to see the condition this guy is in. He was in great shape at the time of the accident (when he was hit head-on by a car), and though he was in critical condition for a while, now he is up early at the gym, working out. I saw him and couldn't help telling him what an inspiration he is to people! The people who inspire me at the gym are not the people who are natural athletes. They are the people who have gained some weight or feel uncomfortable about their body image, but they still come to the gym. My heroes are like the doctor who is rehabilitating himself and working through pain, the people who get up every morning and make an effort to change their bodies, improve their health, develop good habits. It is a struggle every day for them, but those people are the ones I admire.

It's not that I walk around trying to pick someone to encourage; sometimes I just feel *compelled* to compliment or encourage someone. As you read this, think about people in your life who could use an encouraging word. Who are they? In a room crowded with people, who could use an encouraging word? If you asked that question out loud, every hand would go up, and if it didn't, then it should.

What does giving encouragement do? It changes things in people! If it is sincere and appropriate, it has the power to change the course of someone's day, perhaps even their life. Physiologically, receiving encouragement releases dopamine in our brains and makes us feel healthier, uplifts our attitude, and changes the course of our day, especially if we know that the person giving it doesn't want anything from us. You have heard people reply, "Okay, what do you want?!" when you give them a nice compliment. People can sometimes be cynical about being encouraged. Maybe they don't feel worthy or are so used to being unnoticed that it surprises them.

When you give encouragement to others, you also change the course of *your* day. When you offer that up and realize that it touches them, it also touches *you*. Yes—like that Chinese proverb says—someone who encourages others dignifies himself, because it is healing for you as well.

Am I trying to get you to go out and encourage others? Yes, of course! But mostly what I am trying to do is get you to recognize the fact that we need more of this in our communities. This is something we need to consider adding to our day on a regular basis. There are many ways we can encourage other people. It should not come as part of a list of things to accomplish, but sincerely. Be open, and allow yourself to recognize those around you doing a good job, or being kind, or just showing up when it is hard due to their circumstances. Let your heart do the feeling and your mouth do the talking. You will know when. You will know that perfect time—when it is appropriate to say something a person needs to hear. Usually it is at the point you feel gratitude for what they are doing, no matter how small a thing.

Will this change the course of your life? Maybe not, but it can only help. It may seem like a small thing, but it could make a great difference! It might take a little pressure off and allow your attitude to brighten. A sincere and appropriate word of encouragement is something that can change someone's day or at least set it on the right course.

Here is the flip side of this. I heard of a guy years ago who made it a habit that, whenever somebody said something nice to him, he said, "Thank you" in a way that made you feel better because you had spoken to him. An encouraging word has benefits for both the person who receives it and the person who gives it.

Yesterday, when the doctor came into the gym, I talked to him, congratulating him on his progress, acknowledging what a struggle it must be for him and how far he had come. I told him a little bit about the book I was writing, and he was excited about it. I mentioned to him what an inspiration he was to me because of what he had accomplished. I let him know that he does so even without saying anything, that his actions alone inspire and encourage others around him. He said, "Thank you," in such a profound and touching way that I felt encouraged. I guess I felt *dignified*. I felt special for saying that, but then he turned it around. He said, "You know, Kevin, I watch you. I know you, and most people here know you." (We all get to the gym around 4:00 in the morning and get our workouts done because we are morning people or go to work early.) He said, "Kevin, you also encourage and inspire people on a daily basis." I was not exactly surprised, but I was measuring how I felt. When you're writing a book, you are simply more aware of everything that happens—how someone walks or what they say could wind up being an important part of your book.

When he said those encouraging words, I took a mental step backwards and said, "Thank you. That means a lot to me!" We shook hands, and he went to his workout and I to mine. This whole encounter probably took less than two minutes maximum. This ever-so-brief exchange between this inspiring man and me enriched both our lives, and we both appreciated it. An encouraging word goes much further than one might think. You recognize that it will give someone a moment or two of pleasure, but in dignifying *yourself*, it also helps you.

There are plenty of stories about incredible philanthropists in our lifetime—people who have given of their means, given of their time, sacrificed their lives. Mother Theresa comes to mind. There are many who give of their time and money just to help other people. I am pleased to say that my son Kevin started a nonprofit for missionaries and travels throughout the world helping people who are missionaries and supporting what they do. That would not have been my first choice for him—because of the hardships associated with that lifestyle—but I applaud him, and I'm proud of him. I think it's a wonderful thing that he does this. It is his way of making a difference in the world, and I think it is splendid. I am proud of anybody who does that kind of work because I realize I never could.

The other thing about the encouraging word is that we must remember to stay true to ourselves. We have to find a way to give encouragement as part of who we are. It must become second-nature. Some people say they want to reinvent themselves. They want to be taller, shorter, slimmer, prettier, more outgoing, less outgoing, etc. I talk way too much. That's why I thought I should write a book. That way, I could talk the whole time, and then I would be done. In reality, I have all these pages filled, but it was more about listening than talking. As I have learned and watched others give an encouraging word, part of it is about dignifying the deliverer and blessing the person who receives it.

"What if we could do something that affects our lives in a positive way as well as those of the people around us?" I would say this is the way! *Give an encouraging word.* I encourage you, as you read this book, to consider doing that. There are 12 chapters here, including an epilogue, outlining things you can do to make your life and your relationships a little better. Just pick one. Maybe you want to be grateful the rest of your life. Maybe you want to have empathy for people; maybe you want to be a better listener. Maybe you want to give people the benefit of the doubt. Pick one! There's no way you can grab 12 chapters and do all of them at once. Hopefully each will touch you in some way and help you to adopt the principles described. I would encourage you to start by picking one.

Moreover, *take 10*. We are moving too fast; life just gets faster each day. *Hit the pause button and make a better decision. Take 10, hit the pause button*, and *encourage someone* today! You will make their day and yours just a little bit brighter!

CHAPTER 8

Gratitude is the sign of noble souls.
—AESOP

Gratitude

I created an acronym using the words "BE GREAT." "Bravery in leadership," and "Encouragement" were just covered. "G" for "gratitude" begins the next section. The next chapter (9) will be based on "R" for "respect," then (10) on "E" for "empathy," (11) on "A" for "adaptability" and "adversity," and the last (12) on "T" for time and trust, which are the most powerful aspects of BE GREAT.

Gratitude is one of the emotions we can actually self-generate. Gratitude is something we can create by just concentrating on what we want to do with it. In the book (and subsequent movie) *The Secret*, the author talked about "gratitude rocks." The rocks are a reminder to be grateful for the people, places, or things in your life that are good. Even having clean socks is something to be grateful for in our busy world.

You can go and pick out a rock for yourself. Hold this gratitude rock in your hand, and then lay it wherever you can find it in the morning. When you wake up, grab your rock and say five things that you are grateful for. These could be anything, but just state five things. It could be that you see it is a beautiful day outdoors. It could be that you accomplished a task yesterday and you're grateful it's done. It doesn't matter what the five things are, just state five things you are grateful for. When you get out of bed, grab the gratitude rock and name those. This will set the pace for the day and will put your heart in a place of gratitude for the day.

Where does that put us? How does that adjust our minds? Of course, we are going to pause for a moment to look at the beginning of our day. At the end of the day, do the same thing—name five things you have been grateful for during the day. What happened during the course of the day that you are grateful for?

Any time you are in a place of gratitude, you are not in a place of expectation. In a place of gratitude, you are thankful for the simpler things in life. How wonderful it is that you can have that sensation of gratitude! It's not about what is next. It's not about what you need. It's about what you are grateful for *now*. You're not asking for a miracle. You're not *asking* for *anything*. You are just appreciating what you have. What a wonderful place that is to be!

For example, Christmas came out of a place of giving as opposed to a place of getting. Everybody wants this and that—get these foot warmers, get that beautiful car, all these different things. Christmas is not about that; it's about giving.

When we are in a state of gratitude, we are in the perfect place. *Taking 10 deep breaths* takes you to a place of *gratitude*—you can breathe! *Ten steps* to a place of *gratitude*—you can walk! *Ten seconds* to a place of *gratitude*—you are alive and so blessed! So many things can happen while *taking 10* to make our lives just a little bit better—a better choice, a better direction, or a better thought. Instead of yelling at our spouses, how about appreciating and expressing *gratitude* for what they do for you on a daily basis? As opposed to wanting something, why not have *gratitude* for what you already have? How many marriages would be a little stronger if we were all in a place of *gratitude*? It is so simple it seems hard: to be grateful that your spouse cleaned the kitchen, mowed the lawn, fed the kids, vacuumed the house, and changed the oil in the car—well, enough about my wife! Seriously, though, we can all find something to be grateful for.

A place of wanting is a sad and anxious place. We want what we cannot have, and we will never really be happy if we are in a place of wanting as opposed to *gratitude*. It changes things. We all want the latest gadget, the latest iPhone, etc. I saw a commercial on television the other day. Some guy was struggling with a flip phone; then some iPhone Galaxy thing was shown that reads your pulse, tells you when to exercise, when to eat, probably even when to go to the bathroom. For crying out loud! Really, do we need all this? The message was this: *That phone does so much more than the phone you have, you simply must have this phone!*

If instead you are *grateful* for what you have, that would be so much better! There will be some people reading this book right now who can remember when there was a telephone party line. As a kid growing up, our phone number was two letters and some numbers. We had to wait sometimes because somebody else was using the phone. The operator would come on and ask if we could wait a little bit longer so the other party could finish their conversation. I thought that was just normal. I dreamed about how cool it would be to have one of those phones attached to a suitcase…walk around all cool with a little phone, walking around and talking on the phone! That was neat! Before that, I thought a long cord was really cool, but luggage with a phone? Now we have gotten to the point we have a little phone and an earpiece and we can talk to anybody in the world on it. Why not just be *grateful* for that?

Computers are so fast, but we used to have a phone book to look up a number. Now we just talk to Siri (with an Australian accent or another one of your choice) on the phone to be connected to whomever we want. My daughter played with my phone and wanted an English accent but got an Australian one that sometimes I can't even understand!

Everything is happening so fast, but there is still so much to be grateful for. There was a lady in front of me in line recently who was just flabbergasted at how long it was taking to get to the counter. I just engaged her a little bit and said, "Boy, isn't it amazing that all these people are in line and I don't recognize any of them? Do you?"

"Well, no, but they should be faster!" she replied.

How can they be any faster? I thought but said, "Isn't it cool that they are going to help us here pretty soon? Let's just appreciate that."

I'm no genius at this! I am learning as I go. Can I be in a better state of gratitude? You bet! I am surrounded by people who are just absolute blessings to me—my wife being the best example. Some of the things she does for our family, for me, and for the people around her—it is just amazing to me! She is able to go through her day at work and do all the things she does there and still have enough time and energy to raise a family.

Why not be grateful for the people around you? You have good friends who call and check on you when you're sick. A heart in a state of gratitude cannot hold onto any resentment. Our mind and heart, our very essence in a state of gratitude, fills all the holes we have. When we are sincerely grateful, we are thankful for everything. Why do we have to wait until late November every year and take one day out of the year to be thankful and grateful? Why not do it every day?

This chapter is a challenge to each of us, including myself. *Take 10. Try to slow down.* If we continue to be in a state of gratitude, we can overcome a lot of pains and ills in our lives. I truly believe that being grateful for the fact that I have clean socks today is not a stretch—it's a good thing, and I am grateful for it. I'm grateful I have money to buy breakfast, to have a home and family. Those are big things, but I'm grateful for the little things, too.

Wherever your heart is as you are reading this book, I guarantee you that, if you are not already doing it, naming five things you are grateful for each morning is going to start your day off so much better. Then, at night, before you put your head down on the pillow, think of five things you are grateful for at the end of the day. Remember especially your family members (your spouse right next to you or your children in the next room), and you will relax and sleep better.

This, I assure you, is not something that comes easily or naturally to me. But as I write this book, which is not something I do on a regular basis, it challenges me to do that. I will commit to you right now that, before I go to sleep tonight, I will come up with five things I am grateful for, and when I wake up tomorrow, I will have five other things to be grateful for. My wife and I used to do this all the time but got away from it. We know how powerful this is. If you have anything you are grateful for, seek it out, and live your life in a state of gratitude. An *attitude of gratitude* will cancel a lot of ill will. There is no way a heart can stay resentful in the presence of gratitude.

There are lots of books on gratitude that go on and on. The purpose of this book is to make the process simpler so it is easy to perform. There is no magic here, no formula, no mathematical equation. All you have to do is be grateful for what you see and feel. Be grateful for what you have. Don't long for what you don't have. The secret is that, as you realize how grateful you are for what you have, you have more. If you are grateful for all you have, your life is filled with abundance.

Take 10 and *embrace a state of gratitude.* Remember: "Five in the morning and five at night, starts and ends your day just right!"

CHAPTER 9

*Everyone should be respected as an
individual, but no one idolized.*
—ALBERT EINSTEIN

Respect

It is amazing to me that *simple respect* is something that is so often sought after and yet so difficult for some people to attain for their lives. The question I have asked myself for years is, "Who deserves respect?" I'm sure we have all heard a person who says, "You have to *earn* my respect." Most people probably feel that way. I have to break that down because I am analytical and wonder to myself, "Why?" Why are there some people whose respect you have to *earn*? What is happening in that relationship? Is it conditional? Is it something you have to show them you can do so they can respect you in turn? And on what level? Are there different levels of respect?" There is a baseline respect that we all automatically get just for showing up. Let's consider what the motives might be for the person who says, "You have to *earn* my respect." Let's assume for a minute that he is well-meaning and is just trying to be truthful. Maybe he has heard something that predisposes him to feel a certain way about you. Maybe he is hardwired not to respect *anyone*.

Some people see life as a kind of dog-and-pony show. You have to do certain things, talk a certain way, walk a certain way, perform this way. Your job quality has to be just so, or you have to make a certain amount of money, have to drive this type of car. Today society seems to be all about status. Most people are waiting for someone to earn their respect. To me, that puts them in a position of judgment. Who are they to judge whether they ought to get respect or not?

"Respect" might be a misused term. Some people may see "respect" through too narrow a lens—it may be respect only for one's position or job or something else. This narrow focus creates a problem. Respect is just a way of acknowledging that each person has value. Each person is worthwhile. Everybody *deserves* respect, don't you think? Most people don't consciously start every day off thinking about ways they have to earn someone's respect. You deserve respect. Everyone deserves to *start off* with respect for others and being respected by others. You respect the person who is collecting cans, and you respect the person who made the cans in the first place. You respect the distributor of the finished product. You respect the person in the car in front of you, even if they cut you off—you still respect them.

Can you lose someone's respect? I believe you can. If we really want to dignify ourselves and understand what appreciating others means, isn't that the deepest form of respect we can have?

The last chapter was about gratitude, which is such an important thing for all of us. Respect is something that we all desire and all deserve. You can have good days and bad days, and you might make mistakes and poor decisions, but ultimately having respect for each other changes society. It is a lack of respect that changes society for the worse, whether it is for an ethnic class, members of a religion, or a choice made for work. Sometimes we are predisposed to make a judgment against somebody, and just their very existence bothers us. We cannot respect the choices they make. We have to examine the whole idea of respect. We have to look deep inside ourselves.

If there is someone for whom you have no respect, why is that? Was it because of an event? Was it a choice they made? If an event happened, and it is shown they made a poor choice and affected other people negatively, maybe caused harm, how can you respect them? A major story in the news right now is about the doctor who treated female athletes and sexually abused them for years. He caused so much pain to them after they put their lives in his hands! Their parents always intended to take really good care of their daughters—how could they let this happen? None of those involved will ever be quite the same. People will always say about this doctor, "He lost my respect a long time ago!"

What about the people who just made a choice for themselves—one that does not really affect you? If you think you can't respect them, isn't that more your problem than theirs? Anybody on this earth who is doing all they can deserves respect. If they're not doing the best they can, maybe they are having a really tough time. Can't we have a little more compassion for people? Can't we work a little bit harder at looking deep within ourselves to make sure we have respect for each other?

Imagine a place where everyone has mutual respect. Companies like Apple and Toyota seem to have tremendous respect for the workers in their factories. The grandson of the founder of Toyota has a great deal of respect for the people who work for Toyota, not only in the manufacturing areas but also in the dealerships. I have seen this firsthand—a respected individual who *demonstrates* respect and humility. I wish there were an "H" in GREAT, because "humility" is a powerful human trait. I believe having true humility really makes a difference in people.

Respect is an important aspect of our lives. Reach inside, after you name your five reasons why you are grateful for the day, and understand that you are going to have respect for the people around you—respect for the work they do, respect for what they stand for, and respect for the choices they make. Don't worry about whether they measure up to your standards or beliefs; just acknowledge that they are worth respecting! You can respect everyone.

I sometimes have problems myself with this. I am having a hard time understanding some choices that people have made. But who made me judge and jury? Why is it that I get to say why I don't want to talk to this person or deal with them? This is an issue I am working on myself. There are people I run into whom I really have a hard time respecting. Maybe it's not even a question of respect; maybe it's just that I don't understand them.

Maybe we are misusing the word "respect." Maybe it means something different now from what it used to mean. Instead of "respect," maybe we mean "like" or "appreciate." Maybe it's just semantics.

The way I see "respect" is this: If a person is standing in front of you, you shouldn't go out of your way to treat him or her badly. You shouldn't go out of your way to do anything except just appreciate the individual. I believe that dignifies you. Respect is such a powerful word! The act of respect is really the beginning of love. There is no good, strong relationship that does not start with a baseline respect. I sometimes feel bad for the people who walk around all the time thinking others have to *earn* their respect. I wonder if they really know what they are looking for. They put expectations on people and want people to do a certain thing and act a certain way. Are they really looking for *praise* instead of respect? Is it ever enough? If they see a dog-and-pony show right in front of them, is that enough to make them respect the person conducting it? What else would they need? Is it always going to be, "You earned my respect today; we'll see how you do tomorrow."? What does that do to the person who is trying to earn somebody's respect? We respect them automatically because that is how we are built. It's a big challenge if we come to find out that, no matter what we do, it's not going to be enough to "*earn*" their respect.

To respect is to make a choice. Just as *in giving people the benefit of the doubt*, we get to choose how we respond to people. You are in control of how you choose, how you respond, how you respect. You get to make that choice. Remember, we are not better or worse than anyone; we are just different. We are here with different choices, different feelings. I would encourage you to look at that and feel respect. That is something we can always work on.

In the next chapter, we are going to discuss *empathy*, which is a trait that will help us respect people. It is the connection that is lacking. The community I live in is experiencing a rise in the number of people with mental-health issues. Our county has had one of the highest rates of suicide in the nation. Statistics from 2016 and 2017 show no improvement. Depression hits this community pretty hard. One of the main reasons for this book is the love I feel for my community. We have lots of the ability and desire to connect. We need to *take 10* and have *gratitude* and *respect* for each other, *slow down*, and enjoy our beautiful county. Our communities can't continue at this speed. We need to relax and "enjoy our shoes." We need to *slow down* and just enjoy life. We have to *hit the pause button*.

Respecting somebody is just *slowing down enough to look at them and appreciate them*. Each person has something worth appreciating. They aren't necessarily wiser or more gifted; they may not know any more or less than you. They're not a better or worse person than you are; they are just different. Once we level that playing field and respect each other, it is a game-changer for all of us. Respect is important if a society is to move forward, yet it is fleeting and seldom achieved.

Is there a way that we can really jumpstart a community into respecting its members? Philadelphia just won the Super Bowl with a major upset over New England. The city is on fire! It has always been the City of Brotherly Love. What is it about Philadelphia right now? People have a common cause around which to unite and celebrate. People love each other right now in Philadelphia. The whole community has been brought together! Whether it is respect, love, mutual appreciation—if you live in Philadelphia right now, you are part of a major party. The game was a big, big upset that nobody saw coming! The inexperienced replacement quarterback did an amazing job when he took over for a great player. Now everyone in the whole city is in love with each other! Philly cheese steaks for everybody! A big win like that brings people together. I don't know how long it will last, but I love to see members of the community absolutely embracing each other. That's respect, admiration, and appreciation for each other.

We can all do this. A win could be just as simple, yet profound, as a life saved in the hospital. It is a big deal for the family involved, and a common cause for celebration could be a big deal for the community. We need to embrace as many things as we can. Great, positive things are happening around us to allow us to respect each other. Each step involves people worthy of respect—from the ambulance driver who took the patient to the hospital, the paramedics who worked on him in the ambulance, the doctors and nurses who assessed him in the emergency room, and finally those who cared for him during his hospitalization.

Some people are trying to keep their retail stores open and provide convenience and choices for us in our community. They are working hard to provide jobs. The sales representatives work hard to make patrons feel accepted and respected. Whatever the job is, whatever choice they make, let's love and respect that. Let's appreciate the people in front of us. *Take the time* today to walk around and look at people in a different light. *Appreciate* the people right in front of you. See them from a different perspective. *Respect and appreciate* the person who rings up your groceries. *Respect* the person who bags your groceries. They are no more or less than you; they are just different! This is what they are doing. Maybe they are kids going to school or seniors at the end of their working days. Maybe they do this because they love people. *Respect* your neighbors; love your neighbors. Let's respect each other. Let's start *The Respect Revolution.* Picture throwing a rock into the middle of a pond and watching the amazing ripple effect. Let's create that with respect. You be the rock! You be what starts the ripples. You respect your neighbors, and they will respect you, and on and on. Let's start a movement to *respect each other.*

Take 10. Hit the pause button, and respect the person in front of you.

CHAPTER 10

The opposite of anger is not calmness;
it is empathy.
—DR. MEHMET OZ

Empathy

One of the most challenging issues we face is to understand someone else's point of view. Where are they coming from? What circumstances in their lives have made them the way they are? The fact that we spend most of our time with our faces in our phones means we don't look up to see what people are thinking or saying. Making a connection by actually watching people talk and feeling their perspective is no easy task. This is one reason why the divorce rate is so high—we have just stopped listening and communicating with each other.

Forty years in the car business taught me a lot of things. It taught me that you truly can connect with people just by listening and watching. There are all these clues they give you. Tools are available to learn how to spot nonverbal communication and mirror how the customer sits or walks. Watch their breathing; look for microexpressions and how their face moves. Hear what they mean without them actually saying it! It is amazing that you can watch a person closely and really feel what they are feeling. They will tell you. Nonverbal communication and microexpressions are controlled by the subconscious. We cannot tell ourselves to pick up our hand and scratch our chin or look to the left or any of the other clues that might reveal one thing or another. We don't tell our bodies to do those things; our bodies just naturally do them. That is our true self.

How do we make that connection? In the car business, it was important for us to understand, to connect with our customer; that is one of the most important aspects of making a deal. If you have a true connection with your customer, the chances of you being able to close the deal are much higher than if all you are thinking about is, *I need this sale! Let's get on to the next one.*

We go about our everyday lives; we look around and see people. If you have your head up and not buried in your phone but are really watching people, the dance of life you see will amaze you. It's just a wonderful (and simple) way to connect with people—just watching them and feeling them. *Having empathy for someone* is another name for that true connection.

If people sense you have an agenda—such as selling a car or another product, even selling a book—then the connection does not feel real to them. If you want to demonstrate that you truly understand where they are coming from just for the sake of understanding them and wanting to connect with them, then that will be a true connection. Reach out and be their friend or a person who listens to them.

Empathy has always been important to me. Coming from the abusive background I came from, I think there were several things that changed me. One is that I became a keen observer of the obvious. The tinkling of the ice in the glass and the way my father stirred his mixed drink was a pretty good indicator of what kind of mood he was in. We all listened to hear how he walked, to know exactly how he was going to respond, or just what he was going to do. I think a lot of people from abusive backgrounds have the same keen observational skills—they watch people.

Some people love animals; I love people! Some have let me down. Have I let some people down? Absolutely.

There are many things I could have done differently or felt differently about. There are things I have said that I wish I could take back, and there are things I wish people had not said to me. However, at the end of the day, people are amazing! If you embrace that, if you *take 10 breaths, 10 steps, 10 seconds to truly understand the person in front of you and make that connection,* life will be better. Life is always better when we know someone else is dealing with issues similar to ours. If we truly empathize with the person who is next to us, we can have that true connection and learn something from them.

I had a great lunch the other day with a couple of people from a school in town that trains medical technicians, mechanics, and other trade skills. I was amazed at their great understanding of people and appreciative of how much they really cared about their students. There wasn't anything false at all. They really cared about the students being trained for a job, being prepared for a job, and developing a career. They were excited about their students' excitement and accomplishment!

When I first met them, I didn't know exactly what to expect. Once you get to know someone a little and see their passion for what they do, it is exciting and gets you excited about that as well. We are going to be using some of their phlebotomists as we are doing a free health fair. Some of their students are going to be helping us, and it is very exciting.

If we take the time to really reach out to people, that connection will take us to the next level. If we allow ourselves to be open as we talk to other people and try to fully understand where they are coming from, we could get a unique gift, an epiphany, something from them that might make our lives just a little bit better. How great would that be? I fervently believe that it is intended for us as human beings inhabiting this planet to connect with one another. Sometimes you don't want to reach out and talk to people. There are introverted people, there are extroverted people, and then there's me—I'm probably a little too extroverted. It's the connections we make and the people we can empathize with who make our lives rich. The richness comes from the diversity in our lives. It is in that diversity that we can learn more about ourselves as well as others.

Reach out and feel free to care. Don't put yourself in harm's way, of course. There are plenty of times when you reach out to try to connect with someone, and you either get turned away or they take advantage of you. Many of us have had that happen. We could say, "That's great advice, but last time I trusted somebody, I got hurt." Don't give up hope! There are a lot of wonderful people out there, and as you interact with people, *take 10 seconds* to understand where they are coming from, or *take 10 breaths* to relax so you can really connect with them. It could be a life-changing moment for you and for them, and it could be something that helps you grow. There is so much out there for us, and we have the ability to see more, to feel more.

How do we connect with our neighbor? How do you accomplish empathy? You allow them to speak—you let their hearts speak. You let their words permeate your soul and just absorb them. You truly *listen.*

Have you ever had a conversation with a friend at the end of which you felt that you had been really heard? Didn't you feel validated at that point? You might have felt like, "I *do* make a difference. They really *do* care about me!" Isn't it wonderful to have that true connection and really be heard? Sometimes when you're listening to somebody, you have a point you want to make because you think it's a really good point and that it might change how they feel about things. You're so excited! You feel yourself thinking, *"Oooh, ooooh! I want to say something!"* If you're going to be a great listener and have empathy, you have to ride it all the way through to the end. You might forget what you were going to say, but that doesn't matter. You want to know what *their* heart says; you want to understand *their* feelings. What a wonderful thing that is! There is no greater gift than to have empathy and understand someone's heart! When I truly feel listened to, I feel uplifted as I walk away. When people don't care if you are there or not, it has a different effect. At the lunch I talked about, I really felt like both of them listened to me, and I listened to them. That's a great partnership! You don't get that with texting. That's just a brief impersonal, digital conversation, and you don't even get to hear the tone of their voices or see the look on their faces. To really connect deeply with somebody, to develop that empathy, it is vital for us to bond.

The other part of empathy is the ability to relate. We know what other people might be doing in a particular situation, so that gives us a head start. We have been in that situation as well, so we already know how they might be feeling.

As we continue the rest of this journey we are on and *take 10, pause a moment*, and look at your "traveling" companion—maybe literally on a bus or a plane, or maybe figuratively because they are traveling through life with you. Take a moment and just connect. Have empathy for where they are. Understand who they are. It will make your day a lot brighter, and it will really make a difference in theirs.

Take 10 and learn to *empathize*.

CHAPTER 11

*I do believe we are all adaptable, and you're
probably more adaptable than you realize.*
—JULIA LEIGH

Adaptability

We all have the ability to adapt to
our surroundings. We can adapt
to other people. But we all know people who say, "If it
isn't the way I want it, it's not going to happen!" It's fine
to have personal preferences. It's okay to get what you
want, but sometimes we have to be adaptable in order to
help others by accepting that an issue is perhaps more
important to them than it is to us.

Adaptability is a very important characteristic.
Sometimes we have to lean back, make an assessment, *take
10, and hit the pause button* in order to decide whether this

issue is important enough to take a stand on or whether it would be better to adapt to a change. How can we judge what is important to adapt to? How can we judge how important adaptability is in any given situation? That will be different for each of us. Some people seem very flexible and willing to change their positions or even their minds to please others. Conversely, we all know people who are so stubborn that even logic and "proof" cannot convince them that their stance is incorrect.

Picture a young tree with green branches. These branches can bend a great deal without snapping. As the tree grows, the branches become bigger and harder on the outside; they develop tougher bark. Then the branches will not bend as much. If too much force is exerted on them, they will crack and split. They may not break entirely in two, but they will never be the same again. If a young tree grows in a place where the wind is constantly in one direction, the flexibility of the branches is constantly influenced to grow in the direction the wind is blowing.

We all know that we will be influenced by all manner of opinions and events that occur in our lives. The secret is to know oneself and what is truly important in order not to be swayed merely by the strength of someone else's beliefs. We need to be adaptable as we learn new ideas, to embrace the good we encounter and make it part of our own lives. To do so, we have to sift through all the information we are constantly bombarded with and make choices based on our innate beliefs. We will want to accept things that help us grow into better people, but we will want to avoid changing just to please someone else. Other people may have strong opinions; most of us do. Their expression of those opinions is like the constant wind blowing in a particular direction; they are inflexible, and their influence may make us that way, too. The secret is to maintain our inner strength while adapting to the forces around us to the extent that is best for us.

If we are arranging to meet someone for lunch and they propose Chinese food, that's great if you like Chinese food. If, however, you are allergic to MSG, which some Oriental foods contain, then it isn't a good time to adapt to your friend's choice. On the other hand, if you suggest a steak house and you know your friend is vegan, that isn't very considerate. In order to meet with this particular person, you will both have to adapt to find a common ground. It *obviously can* be done—there will be a restaurant that serves food you both will like; it just might take a little effort to find. The best kind of adaptability is mutual.

We all have our preferences and opinions, not to mention our political views! I choose not to discuss politics with anyone I care about because either I will end up offending them or they will offend me. I have never lost friendships over politics, but I have developed aversions to certain people. However, on nonpolitical issues, I have learned a great deal from others; I've even had my mind changed sometimes. Hopefully I have had a positive effect on some people as well.

We all must be adaptable to the weather. Whether it rains or snows or is beautifully bright and sunny, we can't change it. We can adapt to it by wearing warm and/or waterproof clothing or carrying an umbrella, and we can wear sunscreen on bright, cloudless days. If we recognize that people's personalities have their own weather systems, perhaps we can adapt in much the same way.

Sometimes I'm approached by a person who projects black clouds from clear across the room. I don't know who has irritated or hurt him or her, but I can see that something is seriously affecting the person's personality. Hopefully, it wasn't me who caused the pain or offense, but sometimes I have done so unknowingly. Regardless, the first thing I must do is adapt my mood to suit his. I don't mean I will mirror his unhappiness, but neither will I be all sunshine and light. This might make him feel as if I am minimizing his emotions. We all deserve to feel whatever we feel, though we often choose not to show those feelings to everyone else.

If I can begin our conversation by inquiring how he is feeling and perhaps discern why, then maybe I can offer some comfort. He may be undergoing a very difficult time at work or in a relationship, or perhaps he is ill or has suffered a tragedy recently. I can certainly listen and empathize, and perhaps I can bring about some flexibility or improvement in his mood. Maybe things aren't as dark as they seem at that moment. Sometimes another viewpoint is all it takes to bring about a change. Just knowing someone else cares deeply about your situation makes the burden easier to bear as one realizes he can adapt to whatever faces him.

Take 10 and consider how adapting your opinion or mood can help you connect with others in the deepest sense.

Adversity

Y*ou can't end a chapter* on adaptability without mentioning the word "adversity," not just because it starts with the letter "a" and fits the acronym, but also because the most critical time we need to be adaptable is when we face adversity.

I was playing basketball in a city-league game. When we would warm up to play a game, we'd look over at the other team, watch them warm up, and size them up. You watch others do a lay-up—not staring, just kind of casually watching. If a guy is doing a 360-degree dunk, you have to watch, of course! If it is just a lay-up, you're probably going to watch that, too. In one game, I can't remember if we won or lost, but I remember the person I played against. I watched him warm up and was amazed! He had only one hand, and the other was missing from the forearm down. I was just amazed at how comfortably and how easily he did lay-ups and other moves.

Then we went into our huddle and were talking about it. We did mention this particular player; I guess most of the team knew him, though I didn't, as I was relatively new to the area. They were all remarking,

"I hope he doesn't guard me!" It wasn't that they felt bad about playing with him or anything like that. We were all amazed at how adeptly he was moving and shooting with just one hand. We went to line up, and in my mind, though I didn't mention it to anybody, I was saying, "Please, God! Don't let him match up with me!" He was probably about 6 feet 4 inches, lean and athletic, but I did not want him to match up with me. As we were lining up, I heard the fateful words, "I'm going to take the big guy!" Not what I wanted to hear! That was a grueling game! He was all over the place. He stole the ball from me three or four times. The guy was just amazing, and yet he had only one hand, and I had two. I was healthy, but he was also healthy and definitely not "handicapped."

I have seen him around town several times since. I'm always happy to see him, and he's happy to see me. He's very gracious, very loving. He's just a great guy! I remember thinking to myself, *How is it that he can have this kind of attitude and have only one hand?! Surely things are much harder for him with only one hand!* I didn't plan to ask him directly, but the way I approached it was to ask him how he accomplished everything he did. How did he have such an amazing attitude? He replied, "Kevin, I wouldn't know how else to do things! I had to accept the fact that this is where I am and that I grew more during the ordeal."

Adversity is something we all face on different levels. I still have both hands and am able to walk around and do well at different things. It is just amazing to me when I see people who are embroiled in adversity—whether it is a single parent who is working three different jobs to raise their children, teachers who teach special-needs children, or caregivers at assisted-living facilities who must change the diapers of some of the elderly and help them shower and such. Almost everyone is dealing with adversity in one way or another. As I watch some people go through their lives, they may do so without whistling, singing, and dancing, but they accept the challenge and conquer it to the best of their ability. I don't see them begrudging those who are more fortunate. They aren't angry at people who don't have the infirmity, handicap, or the problems that they have. They just embrace where they are and believe things will get better.

Martin Luther King, Jr., said, "The ultimate *measure of a man* is not where he stands in moments of comfort and convenience but where he stands at times of challenge and controversy." So how can we do a better job of handling adversity? The one lesson I learned from my friend with the one hand, the amazing athlete, is that *we are where we are*. Now we have many examples of this. Think about the people who take part in the Paralympics or people coming home from the war in the Middle East who have tremendous struggles just to return to their prewar lives. Do we have to accept the fact that this is our lot in life? Sometimes we do. We have one hand, that's it. We have one leg, that's it.

Maybe the job you have right now really isn't working out, or the boss you work for is just a jerk. All those different things represent the adversity that we face. We wake up, leave for work, and have a flat tire. How do we respond to these things? We just have to *take a moment*, *pause*, and accept that this is where we are *right now*. It does not mean it will be like this all day long. It does not mean we're going to have a bad day. It's only where we are *for the moment*! For the moment, I choose peace and calm. I choose to handle this the way I have watched other people handle adversity—with grace and good will.

My habit for dealing with adversity is that I compare myself to others, and I like to think I become stronger or better or whatever the case is. When I see someone dealing with adversity and doing a great job of it, I say to myself, "How is it they can deal with that situation and I can't even handle a flat tire without losing my temper?" It is what it is *for the moment*. A lot of times the adversities we face are momentary or temporary. The situation will resolve with time one way or another. Will it get worse? It might. Will it get better? Most of the time, it will. We have to wait it out and be patient. We cannot jump to conclusions.

We have teamed adaptability with adversity in this chapter because for us to handle adversity, we have to adapt! We have to be able to adjust to whatever is happening. We must roll with the punches. It comes this way, you go that way! This isn't going well, so try that. This job doesn't work out, go someplace else. It is simple on the surface, but it can be challenging. I worked at a job for 20 years and probably should have left five years earlier, but I didn't. Sometimes people are challenging to work with. You have to accept that maybe you are, too.

The next thing is to ask yourself is to what degree do you have to deal with adversity? Is this something you are bringing upon yourself by choices you are making? Michael Jackson, one of the most amazing entertainers in my lifetime, had a song called "Man in the Mirror." His message was that he was struggling with the man in the mirror. He had to make that man change his ways. Often the adversity we face is because of who we are and what we are doing. We are creating the adversity ourselves. Make sure that you do a checkup from the neck up: Look in the mirror and say, "Is there something I am doing that is making this situation a problem?"

I have recently started a program that is pretty challenging. It is a two-hour meditation each night. Typically I go to bed early because I get up early. As a matter of fact, a lot of this book has been written while sitting in the parking lot at the gym waiting for it to open, or if it is already open, just sitting here taking notes and figuring out the best thing to do. Getting up early like I normally do and having a two-hour meditation at night kind of cuts into the sleeping time, but I have to tell you, it has been a wonderful journey.

The two-hour meditation is challenging for me. I'm kind of a high-energy guy. I don't like to just hang around. I started with a five-minute meditation and thought that was pretty cool—just sit down, cross your legs, sing a couple of "Kumbayas," and then get up and leave. Well, I couldn't do that because I would fall asleep in less than five minutes. Of course, for two hours, there are some times when I am asleep. Sometimes I am awake and thinking about different things. I have been trying to completely eliminate interruptions during this two-hour meditation. Interruptions mean that I am thinking about something else. I have to stop, recenter, and so on.

It has been incredibly healthy and very helpful for me to do this meditation. It really helps me to be centered.

Some of the adversity I was having in my life I generated myself because of errors or mistakes or different choices I had made. Now, with the meditation, I am really working at making sure that I am not creating the problem, that I am the cure for myself. We really do have that power inside. It is important for us to make sure we are not part of the problem. We must have this level of acceptance, to be able to recognize that any given problem may just be momentary in many cases. When it is not just temporary, we must fully accept that. We are all going to face adversity at some point in our lives, perhaps even every day. Our best chance of dealing with it is to be sure to adapt, make sure we are not the problem, make sure that we *pause and take 10.*

The only real way to deal with adversity is to take a step back and ask, "Why is this happening right now?" Doing that is possible only during a pause. We can't take the "Woe is I" approach; that just doesn't work. What is happening that has created this problem? Why am I here? We ask "why?" all the time. Well, why not ask it here?

Adversity is like a fine spice that we add to our lives; it adds richness through challenges. When you have successfully coped with adversity, you come out the other side and realize what you have earned and what you have learned. The position you are in now is probably better. Now you are informed and know you can handle adversity. You are now in the position to say, "I can do this. I can do this thing called *life*. I can make a difference in other people's lives. I can do this! I can raise children. I can work a job. I can help change lives in the world one moment, one day, one life at a time."

I tell my wife all the time, "All we truly have to worry about is today and a little bit of tomorrow." I have been saying that to her since we met. I never really dissected that and don't know why there must be "a little bit of tomorrow" in the saying. Many people say we have to deal only with today. However, there is that little bit of tomorrow that is going to show up as the result of actions taken today. I guess that little bit of tomorrow means that, when you wake up, you have a second chance. When you wake up, what is it that is going on? This can be pretty exciting! Embrace that. Embrace the day! The sunrise at the beginning of the day is just an incredible moment! Embrace those times, and see exactly what we have.

Take 10, and push the pause button to adapt to your adversity.

CHAPTER 12

Dost thou love Life? Then do not squander Time, for that is the stuff Life is made of.
—BENJAMIN FRANKLIN

Time

We're nearly at the end of the road, and this is actually one of my favorite topics in the "BE GREAT" acronym. Do you remember the Jim Croce song from the 1970s called "Time in a Bottle"? In it, he says,

If I could save time in a bottle
The first thing that I'd like to do
Is to save every day
'Til eternity passes away
Just to spend them with you.

Time is so important! It is the only thing we can give to each other that is measured and limited. There is only so much of it to use—24 hours in a day, 12 months in a year. There are only so many moments in a lifetime. It is the most important reason to *take 10* and *hit the pause button*. Stop and realize where you are, what is happening, who you are with, and recognize that you are sharing the precious commodity of time.

If I were to wrap up a gift and have it all ready for you, it would be in beautiful red wrapping paper in a box with a big, beautiful bow on it. You could just lift the top off, and I could present it to you. I like giving gifts, and I like receiving them. The best gift anyone can give to you is their time. That is the one treasure we each have in a finite amount. Once we give it away, it is gone. I hear all the time that there are not enough hours in the day. We are so busy doing so many different things. Sometimes we are busy doing the right things; sometimes we are busy doing the wrong things. Sometimes we are just busy—we multitask, trying to do many different things at once. Research now indicates that multitasking really is not good for us, nor is it as effective as was once thought. We cannot actively use several parts of our brains on different tasks and be successful at all of them. Doing a singular task and getting it done well is more effective. It is satisfying to complete something well.

Albert Einstein said, "You cannot waste time without killing eternity." Are we using our gift wisely? Yes, we all need "downtime" to replenish ourselves, to rest and refuel, but sometimes we get caught up in mindless activities. Oprah Winfrey has said, "I don't waste time because that is wasting myself." How true and poignant these statements are!

Having time and giving it to a friend—just sitting and listening to what they have to say, just *hitting the pause button on life* and *being really present* is a tremendous gift! At the end of their lives, many people might say, "If only I had a little more time! Then I could do the things and say the things to people I want to say." Time is critical. It is so important for us to take the time and cherish those we love, just enjoying the moments we have with them. Time goes by so quickly. I heard a saying once, "Life is like a roll of toilet paper—the closer you get to the end, the faster it goes!" I would have to agree with that. It seems now that one day is nothing; it seems a week is like a day, and a month seems as short as a week. Everything goes by so quickly; one turns around and it is the middle of the year that just started in January!

Time is the only thing we can really share with others. We can give them love and care for them and receive love and care back, but only time can be experienced simultaneously with another person. Mutual experiences can be relived and discussed over and over with whoever was also present. What fun that can be! Yet we all have the ability to stop time in that we have memory. We can experience a sweet or exciting moment over and over again. However, in the same way, we can undergo punishment or embarrassment repeatedly, so we have to choose to avoid negativity in our memories. That's just a waste of time.

Some very efficient people I know are "planners." They make appointments with themselves for rest, to read a book, to exercise, etc. They budget their time down to the last minute. I am less efficient perhaps in that I have rather vague plans of things I would like to accomplish on a given day. That allows for spontaneity in life, but in reality a mixture of both techniques is probably wisest. If I don't make lists, I tend to forget things. I always record planned "official" appointments and refer to my calendar at least once daily. I used to list everything I expected to accomplish during the day, like grocery shopping, putting groceries away, emptying the dishwasher, etc., just so I could cross things off and feel a sense of achievement. I recognize that sometimes I don't use my time wisely, because at the end of the day I can't list a single accomplishment that anyone else would consider important. However, on most days, I talk with people I love who are not present in my home. I learn about their days and how they feel, and we share love, even if it's just over the phone. Those are the truly special times to me.

Young people today are familiar with so many things I expected to be much further in the future than they turned out to be. In many ways, I admire their abilities to use technology, but I see it as frequently tethering them to something with no real value for them. They give up their time to watch someone else experience life on YouTube. They watch others' seemingly perfect lives on Facebook. When I was a child, I played outside all summer. I swam, made forts in the backyard, built treehouses, played with friends, and pretended to be any character I wanted. We used our imaginations to entertain ourselves. We also developed adaptability in that we would come up with the plot of our pretend or imagined future lives together. What memories are the children of today making? When they are old, what will they be able to tell their grandchildren about how they spent their time? If we are in a position to intervene, sometimes we must do so. Let's encourage others to value time; we know how precious it is. It cannot be replaced or refilled. When it's gone, so are we!

Take 10 and learn to *value time*. Share it with those you love most as well as with those you simply encounter in your life.

Trust

The chief lesson I have learned in a long life is that the only way to make a man trustworthy is to trust him; and the surest way to make him untrustworthy is to distrust him and show your mistrust.

—HENRY L. STIMSON

When little babies come into the world (and I have seen four of them born), it's almost as if they are looking for something. Their arms are outstretched. When they open their eyes, they are looking around, trying to figure out who is going to love them. Who is it who brought them here? Who will hold and cuddle them and teach them to ride a bike and throw a ball? Who will show them how to stand proudly at a dance? Babies come into the world and don't know who their parents are. Of course, they are right there—the mother, hopefully the father—holding the baby and wanting to be close to each other. Then 18 years later they are on their way. It seems like such a short time when you look at life in its entirety. You have these babies for

18 years, or in some cases, only 16 or 17 and maybe even a shorter time.

When they are little, babies have no idea other than to trust. They reach out for food, and it comes. They look for warmth, and it is there. They need a diaper change, and it happens. Everything they need is right there when they need it. As they get older and grow up, they don't have any idea how that works; they just know someone was always around and that Mom and Dad loved and cherished them.

What happens to a little baby or a little boy or girl when they are grown up—what happens when the person who was supposed to be taking care of them does something bad to them? What happens when the trust is broken? What happens when they suffer verbal, physical, or sexual abuse at an early age—seven, eight, nine, ten years old—right in critical times of growth?

If you can look in that mirror and see yourself as you read this book, make sure that you talk about it. The one thing that you need most in the world as time passes is someone you can trust. When that is all you know and the principal people in your life have taken that away from you, then how do you get through life? I am going through a major catharsis as I'm writing this book. I alluded to the abuse that happened to me earlier in my life and to my siblings and how my father was the perpetrator and my mother was helplessly watching and standing by while all this happened, possibly dealing with her own demons.

I have to ask myself a question. What is it that creates these people? Is it just a perpetuation of an ill, of a pattern that is passed from one generation to the next? I have always considered myself blessed in a lot of ways because now my oldest son, Kevin, 38 years old with a young son of his own, is doing a wonderful job of parenting. He is a stay-at-home dad, and I am very proud of him. I knelt at the side of my bed, and I asked for help because I knew the pattern of abuse had to stop with me. I said it out loud: "It stops here!" The generations of abuse—who knew what my father and my grandfather had suffered through? But it stopped with me, with my sons, with my brother's son and daughter, and with my new 7-year-old twins. They feel loved and cherished, and they can trust. It is a wonderful thing.

But what about you in the mirror? What happens when that trust is broken? We do have to make sure that we take care of ourselves, and we have to find people we can trust. There are people out there who are worthy of our trust. There are people you can lean on and understand that they are trustworthy. When you go through abuse at an early age, you have no idea that not everybody is like your abuser. You just assume that no adult can be trusted. Throughout my life I have had problems trusting anyone. I didn't know if there was anyone I could actually lean on and trust until I met my current wife. That's not the fault of other relationships I had in the past, but I realized that I had problems with trust then and probably helped to create the mayhem that ensued. I do not know what drives a person to do one thing or another; when you don't trust them, it is hard to say. All I can say is that throughout my life I had problems trusting anyone. Again, if you can see yourself in this mirror, I would encourage you to talk through these issues. Find people you can trust, sit with, and talk to about it and get encouragement to go forward. The inability to trust is an outwardly scarless disease. People do not see it in you. They don't recognize it.

Oprah Winfrey did a series on posttraumatic stress disorder on *60 Minutes*. Oprah suggested that when people act up and don't seem like themselves, someone should ask them, "What happened to you?" "What is your story?" If there is ever a time to *take 10*, it is when you ask somebody that question and they actually have something to talk about. They may be dealing with a lack of trust, that invisible demon within them.

Chapter 12: Time and Trust

Concerning PTSD in general, I am hesitant to say that I have it because I'm just not sure. But when the PTSD is in relation to child abuse, I can raise my hand and say that is me. It may not seem there is enough evidence of it in me, enough scarring, or anything that was severe enough to create PTSD, but yes, there was.

So what happens to us when we can't trust? It turns us into a different person. It isolates us, and we feel like we are an island. We have a hard time communicating. Many people who have been very successful over the years but who lacked trust eventually ended their lives in horrible ways. Robin Williams is a perfect example. I know what kind of life he had when he was growing up. He was extremely funny, probably one of the funniest guys ever to come along—but we can also say that he was haunted. We know he was because he talked a lot about it. He used humor to counteract his demons as well as drugs and alcohol, as do some others. Some abuse victims may become abusers themselves—they display self-injurious behavior or may abuse others. Many coping mechanisms are not good.

It's really important to sit down, talk with somebody, share your feelings, and explain how you feel.

This book has to end on trust because it really is one of the critical factors in *taking time*. We have to trust that there are going to be enough hours in the day to be able to do what we must accomplish. We have to trust that the person sitting in front of us really is interested in what we have to say. We have to trust that our partner is there for us, just as we are there for them. We have to also trust ourselves. These are critical aspects of our lives. Can you honestly say, "Yes, I trust myself, and I trust the people around me"?

What if someone breaks your trust? It is a lot like respect. Are we to assume that we can trust everyone and occasionally (or frequently) be let down, or should we be on guard all the time, with our hands out in front of us and our eyes wide open? Can we trust anyone? Society makes it hard to judge people's motives, but you have to. You have to understand where people are coming from.

I wish I had done a better job trusting up to this point in my life, but I know I can turn it around now because I have identified that invisible demon and am dealing with it. I am going through that catharsis I talked about and trying to empty myself of all the mistrust that has affected my life all these years. Looking back, I recognize how many people I could have trusted and leaned on and did not. Some of the opportunities I missed for friendship or kindred spirits make me sad.

Chapter 12: Time and Trust

Earlier I alluded to the fact that I had lost my scholarship. I signed a letter of intent in my living room when I was 16 years old and a junior in high school. I went to Westmont College in Santa Barbara, California. It is a beautiful college, and the coach was the person in my living room. He said these words to me. "We not only *want* you to come to Westmont, we *need* you to come to Westmont!" I couldn't sign fast enough. My mom was in the kitchen cooking, and my dad was, of course, nowhere to be found when I made one of the most important decisions in my life. As a young man signing that piece of paper, I could not have been prouder because this was a step in the right direction. Getting a four-year scholarship was such a big deal to me, but I had no idea. I figured it was just another stepping stone to the end result. Bring it on!

After two and a half years, the Dean of Boys asked me to his office and then asked me to leave the school because of the culmination in a series of wrong choices I had made. When those emotional floodgates opened following years of repression...let's just say things happened. He asked me to leave because of my reckless abandonment of the school and its principles, and because of my temper. He did not ask what Oprah Winfrey suggested, "What happened to you?" It was the 1970s;

abuse wasn't anything people even thought about. There were too many examples of people with bad tempers and everything else. They just assumed it was my personality, a character flaw.

I remember leaving the campus kind of in a fog. I had to find a job; I had to find a place to live. There were people who helped me, but, of course I didn't trust their motives. It was such a shameful time for me. I had lost the one thing I had worked so hard for my whole life up to that point. Sure, I was a young man, but I had trained for hours just to be able to play well and be part of a team, and I lost that because of lack of trust and lack of focus, because of the invisible demons that drove me. When I think back, I was a happy-go-lucky guy in high school. I was always joking around, often referred to as the Class Clown. I loved to play sports, especially basketball. So what happened in college? And did I know that my newfound anger was intertwined with my childhood trauma?

I've had two failed marriages, and I can't say exactly what my contribution was to those failures. For some reason, I raised my hand for the third one, and thankfully this one saved my life. I can honestly say that my wife, April, and my two beautiful children, Adam and RubyJean, and, of course, my older children, Kevin and

Chris, who are more like my friends and brothers now than my children, all contributed to saving my life. I don't know why, but it was just spinning out of control, and all of a sudden, I ended up someplace I shouldn't have been. We could all be in that position very easily, but trust is what we lean on. Trust is what we try to find, both in others and in ourselves. Trust is that part of us that makes us different.

When you look in the mirror and see yourself, ask yourself this question: "Who do you trust?" Do you trust the man in the mirror? I mentioned Michael Jackson's song about struggling with the man in the mirror. I don't know if he ever really started trusting based on the timing of the song and the circumstances that surrounded it. Maybe he didn't.

I can tell you that I am staring pretty hard at the man in the mirror these days! It's not that there aren't trustworthy people around us, because there are. They are on the treadmill next to you at the gym. They're in the office across the hall. It gets complicated, because the people you would think you could trust—leaders in the church, stalwarts in the community—all of a sudden may surprise you. I don't have any answers for that. I guess it comes down to the respect factor. You have to respect everybody until they cause you to lose respect for them. Who do you trust? Maybe everybody until you learn who you can't! There are enough con artists in the world who are amazing at selling their wares and pulling the wool over your eyes, but they aren't the only people we know. There *are* people we can trust, but I don't know if there is someone you can actually point to and say, "This is a trustworthy person."

A life without trust has not been fun, I can tell you that! Depending on how old you are, if you lack that and then find somebody you can hold on to, they will save your life. They might be right next to you. They could be going to class with you, be the walker or runner next to you, in your homeroom or office. It could be your coach. You don't have to be a person who doesn't trust anyone, because trustworthy folks *are* out there. Just choose wisely and trust!

Trust is love in action. Love represents many things, and trust is one of them. As I write this book and am going through a catharsis, you all have been right alongside me. I appreciate that! I hope you have enjoyed this book and it has meant something to you. I look forward to maybe visiting where you are at some point in time, maybe even being able to meet people who have read the book and learn how it has affected them or helped them in some way.

Chapter 12: Time and Trust

People have told me it takes a lot of courage to put myself out there and let everyone know about the pain and suffering I have had and how I have dealt with it. Some people have told me I am stupid to do that. I think it has been good, for two reasons. First, it is like a giant therapy session. Secondly, if there is a way that hearing about something I suffered through can help someone else, then I am grateful, and I boldly go! In a line from *"Rio Bravo,"* John Wayne tells James Caan, "Ride! Boldly ride!" I am happy to do that because if something I have said helps other people, how can that be bad? I love you all and appreciate your reading this book. I look forward to comments about your feelings on my webpage. *Take 10, and find someone to trust.*

Epilogue

I sincerely hope that reading this has helped you to realize your potential in several areas. First of all, I expect you have learned that *taking 10 seconds, 10 deep breaths, or 10 steps* can help you make better decisions. You have also learned that every individual, including yourself, is worthy of respect. You have become *a better listener and more empathetic* than you were before and are more willing to *give others the benefit of the doubt*. You accept that the *self-talk* in your head must be positive in order for you to succeed in life and be happy. You recognize that each of us has a *genius gift*—something that makes us our most effective self and satisfies our need to excel. In addition, you have learned that *taking baby steps* and not over-reaching will avoid the *snap-back effect*. You know that fear and selfishness cannot exist in a heart full of *gratitude*. You realize that we must be *adaptable* in our ever-changing world in order to avoid becoming "broken" when faced with *adversity*. Most of all, you have become cognizant of the *value of time*, that it is limited and cannot be recovered once it's gone. You know it is the single, most meaningful gift we can share with others. You have learned that *trust* can be earned but really must be given freely. May you have a happy, fulfilled life going forward, and may these simple little steps help you achieve that.

> *The unique and richness of our society*
> *lies within our diversity.*
> —KEVIN L. BARCLAY

Book him today!

Prather Marketing
Nona Prather
(918) 809-3977
nona@prather-marketing.com

Life Coach   Author   Speaker